Windows Registry Uncovered

Simplifying the Complexities of Your PC

By

Dr Issa Ngoie

1. Introduction to Windows Registry: Understanding the Core Components

2. Getting Started with Windows Registry: Navigating and Editing Keys and Values

3. Troubleshooting Windows Registry: Identifying and Fixing Common Errors and Issues

4. Optimizing Windows Registry: Maximizing System Performance and Speed

5. Advanced Windows Registry Techniques: Customizing and Fine-tuning Your PC

Contents

Chapter 1: History of Windows

Windows is a series of operating systems developed by Microsoft Corporation. Here is a brief overview of the history of Windows:

- **Windows 1.0**: Released in 1985, Windows 1.0 was Microsoft's first attempt at a graphical user interface (GUI) for the PC. It allowed users to run multiple programs at once, as well as use a mouse to navigate the system.

- **Windows 2.0**: Released in 1987, Windows 2.0 introduced a number of new features, including improved graphics, expanded memory support, and the ability to overlap windows.

- **Windows 3.0**: Released in 1990, Windows 3.0 was a major milestone for Microsoft. It introduced a new user interface with improved graphics, as well as support for virtual memory and improved networking capabilities.

- **Windows 95**: Released in 1995, Windows 95 was a significant upgrade over previous versions of Windows. It introduced the Start menu, taskbar, and other features that would become iconic elements of the Windows interface. It also added support for long filenames, plug and play hardware, and 32-bit applications.

- **Windows 98**: Released in 1998, Windows 98 was a refinement of Windows 95. It introduced improved hardware support, including support for USB devices and DVD drives.

- **Windows 2000**: Released in 2000, Windows 2000 was aimed at business users. It introduced improved security features and stability, as well as support for Active Directory and other enterprise-level features.

- **Windows XP**: Released in 2001, Windows XP was a major overhaul of the Windows interface. It introduced a more colorful and streamlined look, as well as new features such as System Restore and Windows Media Player.

- **Windows Vista**: Released in 2006, Windows Vista introduced a new Aero user interface, improved security features, and enhanced search capabilities. However, it was criticized for being slow and resource-intensive.

- **Windows 7**: Released in 2009, Windows 7 was a refinement of Windows Vista. It introduced improved performance and stability, as well as new features such as Jump Lists and Libraries.

- **Windows 8**: Released in 2012, Windows 8 was a major departure from previous versions of Windows. It introduced a new touch-based interface and a new app store, but was criticized for its steep learning curve and lack of support for traditional desktop applications.
- Windows 10: Released in 2015, Windows 10 is the current version of Windows. It reintroduced the Start menu and improved support for touch-based devices. It also introduced new features such as Cortana, Microsoft Edge, and the ability to run universal apps across multiple devices.

Windows Registry history

The **Windows Registry** was first introduced with Windows 3.1 in 1992. It was developed as a central repository for all configuration settings and options for the operating system and the installed software. Prior to the registry, configuration settings were scattered across various configuration files.

In Windows 95, the Windows Registry was expanded to include support for 32-bit applications and the plug and play feature. The registry became a crucial component of the operating system, and any changes made to it could have significant impacts on the system's stability and performance.

With Windows 98, the registry was further expanded to include support for Unicode, enabling the use of non-Latin characters. Windows 2000 and Windows XP saw further enhancements, including improvements to the security and permissions model of the registry.

Windows Vista introduced the concept of registry virtualization, which allowed legacy applications to write to the registry without requiring administrative privileges. Windows 7 continued to build upon this feature, along with improvements to performance and reliability.

Today, the Windows Registry remains a critical component of the Windows operating system and is still used to store and manage configuration settings for the system and installed software.

The Windows Registry, on the other hand, is a hierarchical database that stores configuration settings for the operating system and installed software. It is used to store information such as user preferences, system settings, hardware configurations, and application settings. The registry can be accessed and modified using the Registry Editor tool, which is included with Windows.

While Windows provides the user interface and functionality of the operating system, the Windows Registry provides the underlying settings and configurations that make the system and applications function correctly. Changes to the registry can have a significant impact on the stability and performance of the system, so it is important to exercise caution when making modifications.

An operating system like Windows uses the Windows Registry to store and manage a wide range of configuration settings and options for both the operating system itself and any installed software. Here are a few ways that an operating system might utilize the Windows Registry:

1. **System settings**: The operating system stores a variety of settings and configuration options in the registry, such as settings for the desktop background, power settings, and network settings.

2. **Hardware configurations**: Windows uses the registry to keep track of hardware devices connected to the system, their drivers, and associated settings.

3. **Application settings**: Installed software often stores configuration settings in the registry. For example, Microsoft Office stores various settings and preferences in the registry.

4. **User profiles:** Windows stores user-specific settings, preferences, and configurations in the registry. This includes user account information, desktop settings, and application preferences.

5. **Performance settings**: The Windows Registry can be used to optimize the performance of the system. This includes settings related to memory management, disk cache size, and other system-level performance optimizations.

In short, the Windows Registry is a central repository for configuration settings and options for both the operating system and installed software. It allows the operating system to efficiently manage and retrieve system settings and configurations, as well as provide a centralized location for users and administrators to view and modify system configurations.

Why windows registry ?

The Windows Registry was created as a central repository for configuration settings and options for both the operating system and installed software. Here are a few reasons why the Windows Registry is used:

1. **Centralized configuration management**: The Windows Registry allows all software applications to store their settings in a central location. This makes it easier to manage configurations, as administrators and users can view and modify settings for multiple applications in a single place.

2. **Efficient access to configuration data**: The Windows Registry provides a fast and efficient way for the operating system and software applications to access configuration data. This is because the registry is loaded into memory when the system boots up, and software can access the data without needing to read from multiple configuration files.

3. **Customization**: The Windows Registry provides a powerful way to customize the operating system and installed software. Users and administrators can modify registry settings to tweak system behavior, optimize performance, and customize the look and feel of the system.

4. **Debugging**: The Windows Registry can be used to help troubleshoot issues with the operating system and installed software.

By examining the values stored in the registry, administrators can identify and fix configuration-related issues that might be causing problems.

How devices use windows registry?

*D*evices, such as printers, scanners, and other hardware peripherals, can use the Windows Registry to store configuration settings and other information related to their operation. Here are a few ways that devices use the Windows Registry:

1. **Device driver installation**: When a device is installed, its device driver typically adds information to the Windows Registry to specify the device's settings, capabilities, and other configuration information. This allows the operating

system and other software applications
to communicate with the device and
take advantage of its features.

2. **Configuration settings**: Devices can also
store configuration settings in the
Windows Registry, such as preferences
for print quality, network settings, and
other options. This information is used
by the operating system and other
software applications to interact with
the device in a consistent and reliable
way.

3. **Troubleshooting**: The Windows Registry
can be used to help troubleshoot issues
with devices. For example,
administrators can examine the values
stored in the registry to identify and
diagnose problems with a device, such as
driver conflicts or configuration errors.

4. **Plug and Play**: Devices that support the Plug and Play (PnP) protocol can use the Windows Registry to communicate with the operating system and other software applications to automatically configure and manage the device. This can help simplify the installation and operation of devices, particularly for users who are not technically proficient.

how to master windows registry ?

Mastering the Windows Registry can take some time and effort, but here are some steps you can take to get started:

1. **Understand the basics**: Start by learning the basics of the Windows Registry, including its structure, how it works, and its role in the Windows operating system. You can find plenty of resources

online, including articles, tutorials, and videos, that can help you get up to speed.

2. **Use the Registry Editor**: The Registry Editor is the built-in tool for editing the Windows Registry. You can access it by typing "regedit" into the Start menu or Run dialog box. Take some time to familiarize yourself with the Registry Editor, including how to navigate through the registry, search for keys and values, and modify registry entries.

3. **Backup the Registry**: Before making any changes to the Windows Registry, it's important to backup the registry to avoid potential data loss or other problems. You can backup the registry using the Registry Editor's Export feature or by using a third-party registry backup tool.

4. **Experiment with simple changes**: Start with simple changes, such as changing the desktop background or disabling startup programs, to get a feel for how the Windows Registry works. This can help you build confidence and gain experience with the registry.

5. **Read the documentation**: The Microsoft documentation on the Windows Registry is extensive and can provide a wealth of information on how to use the registry. Make sure to read the documentation to learn about advanced features, security considerations, and best practices for managing the Windows Registry.

6. **Practice good habits**: Finally, it's important to practice good habits when working with the Windows Registry. This includes backing up the registry before making changes, being careful when

editing registry entries, and avoiding
making unnecessary or risky changes to
the registry.

windows registry benefits

The Windows Registry provides several

benefits for the Windows operating system and
installed software applications. Here are some
of the key benefits of using the Windows
Registry:

1. **Centralized configuration management**:
   The Windows Registry provides a
   centralized location for all software
   applications to store their configuration
   settings. This makes it easier for
   administrators and users to manage
   configurations, as they can view and

modify settings for multiple applications in a single place.

2. **Fast and efficient access to configuration data**: The Windows Registry is loaded into memory when the system boots up, which provides fast and efficient access to configuration data for the operating system and software applications. This allows the system to access configuration data without needing to read from multiple configuration files, which can improve system performance.

3. **Customization**: The Windows Registry provides a powerful way to customize the operating system and installed software. Users and administrators can modify registry settings to tweak system behavior, optimize performance, and customize the look and feel of the system.

4. **Debugging**: The Windows Registry can be used to help troubleshoot issues with the operating system and installed software. By examining the values stored in the registry, administrators can identify and fix configuration-related issues that might be causing problems.

5. **Scalability**: The Windows Registry is designed to be scalable and can handle large amounts of configuration data for multiple applications. This makes it well-suited for use in enterprise environments, where multiple applications need to be managed across multiple computers.

Chapter 2 : Introduction to Windows Registry: Understanding the Core Components

The Windows Registry is a critical component of the Windows operating system. It serves as a central repository for configuration data and settings for both the operating system and installed software applications. In this chapter, we will introduce the core components of the Windows Registry and explain how they work together to manage configuration data.

First, let's define some important terms. The Windows Registry is a hierarchical database that stores configuration settings and options for the Windows operating system and installed software applications. The database is organized into keys, which are like folders, and values, which are like files within those folders. Keys can contain subkeys, which can contain additional keys and values.

How to open the Windows registry?

To open the Windows registry, follow the steps below for your version of Windows.

Windows 11

1. On the Windows taskbar, click the magnifying glass icon.

2. In the text field at the top of the search window, type **regedit** and press `Enter`.

3. If prompted by User Account Control, click **Yes** to open the Registry Editor.

4. The Windows Registry Editor window should open and look similar to the example shown below.

Windows 10

1. Type **regedit** in the Windows search box on the taskbar and press **Enter**.

2. If prompted by User Account Control, click **Yes** to open the Registry Editor.

3. The Windows Registry Editor window should open and look similar to the example shown below.

Windows 8

1. Type **regedit** on the Start screen and select the *regedit* option in the search results.

2. If prompted by User Account Control, click **Yes** to open the Registry Editor.

3. The Windows Registry Editor window should open and look similar to the example shown below.

The Windows Registry is a collection of databases of configuration settings for Microsoft Windows <u>operating systems</u>.

> The Windows Registry is composed of several key components, including:

Hives: Hives are the highest level of organization in the Windows Registry. Each hive represents a portion of the registry and is stored in a separate file on the file system. There are five main hives: HKEY_CLASSES_ROOT, HKEY_CURRENT_USER, HKEY_LOCAL_MACHINE, HKEY_USERS, and HKEY_CURRENT_CONFIG.

What Is the Windows Registry Used For?

This part of Windows stores much of the

information and settings for software

programs, hardware devices, user preferences,

and operating system configurations.

For example, when a new program is

installed, a new set of instructions and file

references may be added to the registry in a

specific location for the program, and others that may interact with it, to refer to for more information like where the files are located, which options to use in the program, etc.

In many ways, the registry can be thought of as a kind of DNA for the Windows operating system.

It's not necessary for all Windows applications to use the Windows Registry. Some programs store their configurations in XML or other types of files instead of the registry, and others are entirely portable and store their data in an executable file.

How to Access the Windows Registry

The Windows Registry is accessed and configured using the Registry Editor program, a free registry editing utility included by default with every version of Microsoft Windows going back to Windows 95.

Registry Editor isn't a program you download. Instead, it can be accessed by executing **regedit** from the Command Prompt or from the search or Run box from the Start menu.

This editor is the face of the registry and is the way to view and make changes to the registry, but it's not the registry itself. Technically, the registry is the collective name for various database files located in the Windows installation directory.

How to Use the Windows Registry

The registry contains registry values (which are instructions), located within registry keys (folders that contain more data), all within one of several registry hives (folders that categorize all the data in the registry using subfolders). Making changes to these values and keys change the configuration that a particular value controls.

How to Add, Change, & Delete Registry Keys & Values

Making changes to registry values solves a problem, answers a question, or alters a program in some way:

The registry is constantly referenced by Windows and other programs. When you make changes to nearly any setting, changes are also made to the appropriate areas in the registry, though these changes are sometimes not realized until you reboot the computer.

Considering how important the Windows Registry is, backing up the parts of it you're changing, *before you change them*, is very important. Registry backup files are saved as REG files.

Windows Registry Availability

The Windows Registry and the Microsoft Registry Editor program are available in nearly every Windows version including <u>Windows 11</u>, <u>Windows 10</u>, <u>Windows 8</u>, <u>Windows 7</u>, <u>Windows Vista</u>, <u>Windows XP</u>, Windows 2000, Windows NT, Windows 98, and Windows 95.

Even though the registry is available in almost every Windows version, some very small differences do exist between them.

The registry has replaced autoexec.bat, config.sys, and nearly all the <u>INI files</u> that contained configuration information in MS-DOS and in very early versions of Windows.

Where Is the Windows Registry Stored?

The SAM, SECURITY, SOFTWARE, SYSTEM, and DEFAULT registry files, among others, are stored in newer versions of Windows (Windows XP through Windows 11) in this <u>System32</u> folder:

> %SystemRoot%\System32\Config\

Older versions of Windows use the **%WINDIR%** folder to store registry data as <u>DAT</u> files. Windows 3.11 uses only one registry file for the entire Windows Registry, called **REG.DAT.**

Windows 2000 keeps a backup copy of the <u>HKEY LOCAL MACHINE</u> System key that it uses to troubleshoot a problem with the existing one.

Windows registry shorthand and abbreviations

In some documentation and online forums, the registry values may be abbreviated. For example, instead of saying "HKEY_LOCAL_MACHINE," it is easier to say and write "HKLM."

Windows Registry is a hierarchical database that stores configuration settings and options on Microsoft Windows operating systems. It contains settings for low-level operating system components as well as the applications running on the platform: the kernel, device drivers, services, SAM, user interface, and third-party applications all make use of the registry. The registry also provides a means to access counters for profiling system performance.

The registry contains two basic elements: **keys** and **values.**

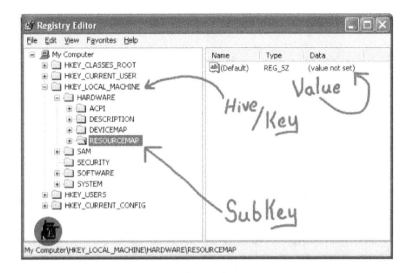

keys and values.

In the Windows Registry, keys and values are the basic building blocks used to organize and store configuration data for the operating system and installed software applications.

A key is a container object that can hold one or more subkeys, as well as values and additional data. Keys are organized hierarchically in the registry, with each key represented by a unique path that includes its parent keys. For example, the path

"HKEY_LOCAL_MACHINE\SOFTWARE\Microsoft" represents a key named "Microsoft" that is a subkey of the "SOFTWARE" key, which in turn is a subkey of the "HKEY_LOCAL_MACHINE" hive.

Values are data objects that store specific configuration settings within a key. Each value has a name, a type, and a data field. The name is used to identify the value within the key, while the type specifies the data format used by the value. There are several value types available in the Windows Registry, including:

1. **String values**: These store text data and can be used to store a wide range of configuration settings, such as file paths, user names, and more.

2. **Binary values**: These store binary data, such as configuration settings for hardware devices.

3. **DWORD values**: These store 32-bit numerical data, such as configuration settings for system settings and performance options.

4. **QWORD values**: These store 64-bit numerical data, such as configuration settings for high-performance computing and gaming.

5. **Multi-string values**: These store text data in a list format and can be used to store configuration settings that require multiple entries, such as the list of installed software applications.

6. **Expandable string values**: These store text data that can be expanded to include environment variables and other dynamic data.

Together, keys and values provide a powerful way to organize and store configuration data in the Windows Registry. By using the Windows Registry Editor, users and administrators can view and modify keys and values to manage the configuration of the operating system and installed software applications.

The registry contains two basic elements: **keys** and **values.**

Registry Keys

Registry keys are similar to folders — in addition to values, each key can contain subkeys, which may contain further subkeys, and so on. Keys are referenced with a syntax similar to Windows' path names, using backslashes to indicate levels of hierarchy. Each subkey has a mandatory name, which is a non-empty string that cannot contain any backslash or null character and whose letter case is insignificant.

The hierarchy of registry keys can only be accessed from a known root key handle (which is anonymous but whose effective value is a constant numeric handle) that is mapped to the content of a registry key preloaded by the kernel from a stored "hive" or to the content of a subkey within another root key or mapped to a registered service or DLL that provides access to its contained subkeys and values.

HKEY_LOCAL_MACHINESoftwareMicrosoftWindows refers to the subkey "Windows" of the subkey "Microsoft" of the subkey "Software" of the HKEY_LOCAL_MACHINE root key.

There are seven predefined root keys:

> ➢ HKEY_LOCAL_MACHINE or HKLM
>
> ➢ HKEY_CURRENT_CONFIG or HKCC (only in Windows 9x/ME and NT-based versions of Windows)
>
> ➢ HKEY_CLASSES_ROOT or HKCR
>
> ➢ HKEY_CURRENT_USER or HKCU
>
> ➢ HKEY_USERS or HKU
>
> ➢ HKEY_PERFORMANCE_DATA (only in NT-based versions of Windows, but invisible in the Windows Registry Editor)
>
> ➢ HKEY_DYN_DATA (only in Windows 9x/ME, and visible in the Windows Registry Editor)

Like other files and services in Windows, all registry keys may be restricted by access control lists (ACLs) depending on user privileges, security tokens acquired by applications, or system security policies enforced by the system. (These restrictions may be predefined by the system itself, and configured by local system administrators or by domain administrators). Different users, programs, services, or remote systems may only see some parts of the hierarchy or distinct hierarchies from the same root keys.

HKEY_LOCAL_MACHINE (HKLM)

The key located by HKLM is actually not stored on disk but maintained in memory by the system kernel in order to map all other subkeys. Applications cannot create any additional subkeys. On NT-based versions of Windows, this key contains four subkeys, "SAM", "SECURITY", "SYSTEM", and "SOFTWARE", that are loaded at boot time within their respective files located in the

%SystemRoot%System32config folder. A fifth subkey, "HARDWARE", is volatile and is created dynamically, and as such is not stored in a file (it exposes a view of all the currently detected Plug-and-Play devices). On Windows Vista, Windows Server 2008, Windows Server 2008 R2, and Windows 7, a sixth subkey is mapped in memory by the kernel and populated from boot configuration data (BCD).

HKLMSAM Key

This key usually appears as empty for most users (unless they are granted access by administrators of the local system or administrators of domains managing the local system). It is used to reference all "Security and Accounts Management" (SAM) databases for all domains into which the local system has been administratively authorized or configured (including the local domain of the running system, whose SAM database has stored a subkey also named "SAM": other subkeys will be created as needed, one for each supplementary domain).

Each SAM database contains all built-in accounts (mostly group aliases) and configured accounts (users, groups, and their aliases, including guest accounts and administrator accounts) created and configured on the respective domain, for each account in that domain, it notably contains the user name which can be used to log on that domain, the internal unique user identifier in the domain, their cryptographically hashed password on that domain, the location of storage of their user registry hive, various status flags (for example if the account can be enumerated and be visible in the logon prompt screen), and the list of domains (including the local domain) into which the account was configured.

HKLMSECURITY Key

This key usually appears empty for most users (unless they are granted access by users with administrative privileges) and is linked to the Security database of the domain into which the current user is logged on (if the user is logged on the local system domain, this key will be linked to the registry hive stored by the local machine and managed by local system administrators or by the builtin "System" account and Windows installers). The kernel will access it to read and enforce the security policy applicable to the current user and all applications or operations executed by this user. It also contains a "SAM" subkey which is dynamically linked to the SAM database of the domain onto which the current user is logged on.

HKLMSYSTEM Key

This key is normally only writable by users with administrative privileges on the local system. It contains information about the Windows system setup, data for the secure random number generator (RNG), the list of currently mounted devices containing a file system, several numbered "HKLMSYSTEMControl Sets" containing alternative configurations for system hardware drivers and services running on the local system (including the currently used one and a backup), an "HKLMSYSTEMSelect" subkey containing the status of these Control Sets, and an "HKLMSYSTEMCurrentControlSet" which is dynamically linked at boot time to the Control Set which is currently used on the local system. Each configured Control Set contains:

- "Enum" subkey enumerating all known Plug-and-Play devices and associating them with installed system drivers (and storing the device-specific configurations of these drivers).
- "Services" subkey listing all installed system drivers (with non-device-specific configuration, and the enumeration of devices for which they are instantiated) and all programs running as services (how and when they can be automatically started).
- "Control" subkey organizing the various hardware drivers and programs running

as services and all other system-wide configurations.

- "Hardware Profiles" subkey enumerating the various profiles that have been tuned (each one with "System" or "Software" settings used to modify the default profile, either in system drivers and services or in the applications) as well as the "Hardware ProfilesCurrent" subkey which is dynamically linked to one of these profiles.

HKLMSOFTWARE Subkey

This key contains software and Windows settings (in the default hardware profile). It is mostly modified by application and system installers. It is organized by software vendor (with a subkey for each), but also contains a

"Windows" subkey for some settings of the Windows user interface, a "Classes" subkey containing all registered associations from file extensions, MIME types, Object Classes IDs and interfaces IDs (for OLE, COM/DCOM, and ActiveX), to the installed applications or DLLs that may be handling these types on the local machine (however these associations are configurable for each user, see below), and a "Policies" subkey (also organized by vendor) for enforcing general usage policies on applications and system services (including the central certificates store used for authenticating, authorizing or disallowing remote systems or services running outside of the local network domain).

HKEY_CURRENT_CONFIG (HKCC)

This key contains information gathered at runtime; information stored in this key is not permanently stored on disk, but rather regenerated at boot time. It is a handle to the key "HKEY_LOCAL_MACHINESystemCurrentControlSetHardware ProfilesCurrent", which is initially empty but populated at boot time by loading one of the other subkeys stored in "HKEY_LOCAL_MACHINESystemCurrentControlSetHardware Profiles".

HKEY_CLASSES_ROOT (HKCR)

This key contains information about registered applications, such as file associations and OLE Object Class IDs, tying them to the applications used to handle these items. On Windows 2000 and above, HKCR is a compilation of user-based HKCUSoftwareClasses and machine-based HKLMSoftwareClasses. If a given value exists in both of the subkeys above, the one in HKCUSoftwareClasses takes precedence. The design allows for either machine- or user-specific registration of COM objects. The user-specific classes hive, unlike the HKCU hive, does not form part of a roaming user profile.

HKEY_USERS (HKU)

Contains subkeys corresponding to the HKEY_CURRENT_USER keys for each user profile actively loaded on the machine, though user hives are usually only loaded for currently logged-in users.

HKEY_CURRENT_USER (HKCU)

This key stores settings that are specific to the currently logged-in user. The HKCU key is a link to the subkey of HKEY_USERS that corresponds to the user; the same information is accessible in both locations. On Windows NT-based systems, each user's settings are stored in their own files called NTUSER.DAT and USRCLASS.DAT inside their own Documents and Settings subfolder (or their own Users subfolder in Windows Vista and Windows 7). Settings in this hive follow users with a roaming profile from machine to machine.

HKEY_PERFORMANCE_DATA

This key provides runtime information into performance data provided by either the NT kernel itself or running system drivers, programs, and services that provide performance data. This key is not stored in any hive and not displayed in the Registry Editor, but it is visible through the registry functions in the Windows API, or in a simplified view via the Performance tab of the Task Manager (only for a few performance data on the local system) or via more advanced control panels (such as the Performances Monitor or the Performances Analyzer which allows collecting and logging these data, including from remote systems).

HKEY_DYN_DATA

This key used only on Windows 95, Windows 98, and Windows Me. It contains information about hardware devices, including Plug and Play and network performance statistics. The information in this hive is also not stored on the hard drive. The Plug and Play information is gathered and configured at startup and is stored in memory.

Values

Registry values are name/data pairs stored within keys. Registry values are referenced separately from registry keys. Each registry value stored in a registry key has a unique name whose letter case is not significant. The Windows API functions that query and manipulate registry values take value names separately from the key path and/or handle that identifies the parent key. Registry values may contain backslashes in their name but doing so makes them difficult to distinguish from their key paths when using some legacy Windows Registry API functions (whose usage is deprecated in Win32).

The terminology is somewhat misleading, as each registry key is similar to an associative array, where standard terminology would refer to the name part of each registry value as a "key". The terms are a holdout from the 16-bit registry in Windows 3, in which registry keys could not contain arbitrary name/data pairs, but rather contained only one unnamed value (which had to be a string). In this sense, the entire registry was like a single associative array where the registry keys (in both the registry sense and dictionary sense) formed a hierarchy, and the registry values were all strings. When the 32-bit registry was created, so was the additional capability of creating multiple named values per key, and the meanings of the names were somewhat distorted. For compatibility with the previous behavior, each registry key may have a "default" value, whose name is the empty string.

CHAPTER 2 : GETTING STARTED WITH WINDOWS REGISTRY: NAVIGATING AND EDITING KEYS AND VALUES

The Windows Registry is a powerful tool that allows users and administrators to manage configuration data for the operating system and installed software applications. To get started with the Windows Registry, you will need to learn how to navigate and edit keys and values using the Windows Registry Editor.

Creating, Editing, or Deleting Registry Keys (Reg Keys) and/or String Values

Issue

You need to create a new Registry Key (Reg Key) and/or string value, or you need to edit or delete one or more of the Reg Keys.

Important note: DO NOT edit or delete Reg Keys from your computer unless you are specifically instructed to do so by one of our Knowledge Base articles or technical support personnel.

Reg Keys are essentially folders that allow Windows applications to process data. On rare occasions, programs such as AutoCAD can become corrupted and require you to delete one or more of these folders. Some functions of our software may also require you to edit a Reg Key.

Solution

Open the Registry Editor

1. Open the Windows **Run** dialog box by pressing the **Windows** + R keys (Windows keyboard) or **Command** + R keys (Mac keyboard).

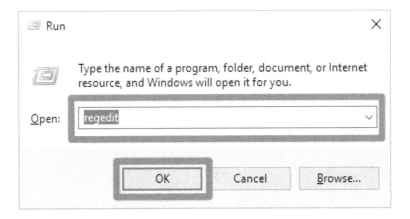

2. In the **Run** dialog box, type **Regedit** and click **OK**.

3. The **Registry Editor** dialog box will open.

The Reg Keys are located within the folders with names that begin with **HKEY_** (as pictured to the right).

A Reg Key's name consists of its folder path within this folder structure.

Some of our troubleshooting articles will instruct you to _edit_ or _delete_ one or more Reg Keys. To locate a Reg Key, expand the first folder in that Reg Key's name (example: **HKEY_LOCAL_MACHINE**) by clicking the right-facing arrow to the left of that folder.

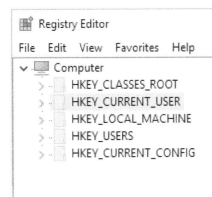

4. Continue expanding folders to locate the Reg Key you need to create, edit, or delete.

Create a Reg Key

To create a new Reg Key, *right-click* the key location where you want to create the new key. Hover the mouse on the **New** option in the menu that opens, then select **Key** from the submenu that opens after that.

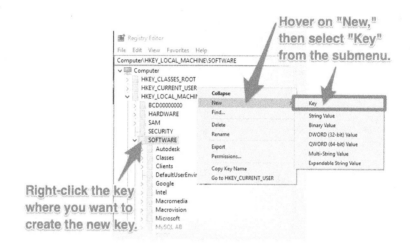

In this example, we'll create a key named **Ecografx** in the key location **HKEY_LOCAL_MACHINE\SOFTWARE**

You'll see a new key within the key path you right-clicked.

Type a name for the key (example: **Ecografx**).

To continue adding keys to the path you've created – for example, if you need to create the key path **HKEY_LOCAL_MACHINE\SOFTWARE\Eco grafx\Land F/X** in following our Manual Installation of the Land F/X Workstation steps, repeat these steps, *right-clicking* the new key you just created and selecting the option for the new key in the menu.

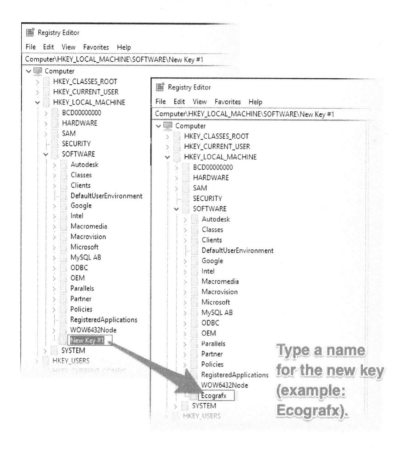

If our Knowledge Base or one of our support technicians has instructed you to create a key path that ends with a string value, move on to the Create a String Value steps below once you've created the necessary key path. So, for example, if you're following our Manual Installation of the Land F/X Workstation

Installer steps, you'd create the key path HKEY_LOCAL_MACHINE\SOFTWARE\Eco grafx\Land F/X and then create the string value InstallPath within the Land F/X key as shown below.

Create a String Value

Creating a string value is similar to creating a key — *right-click* on the key where you want to create the string value, hover on New in the menu, and then select String Value from the submenu. In this example, we'll create the string value InstallPath within the key Land F/X.

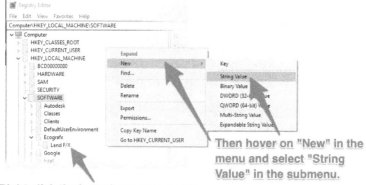

Right-click the key where you want to create the string value (example: Land F/X).

Then hover on "New" in the menu and select "String Value" in the submenu.

The new string value will appear to the right of the key you right-clicked. Type a name for the new string value (example: **InstallPath**)

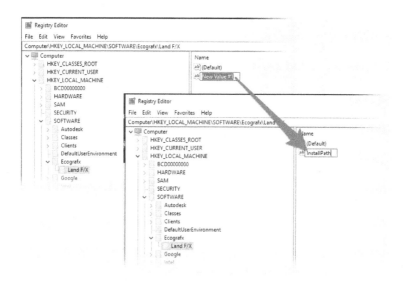

Edit a Reg Key or String Value

To edit a Reg Key or string value, click the Reg Key folder to open it. In our example, we'll edit the Reg Key **HKEY_LOCAL_MACHINE\SOFTWARE\ODBC\ODBC.INI\LANDFX** by clicking the folder **LANDFX** in the path of the same name.

In the right pane, you'll see a list of files, or "strings," contained within the Reg Key you selected. *Right-click* the string you want to edit. Select **Modify** from the menu that opens. In our example, we'll edit the string **SERVER**.

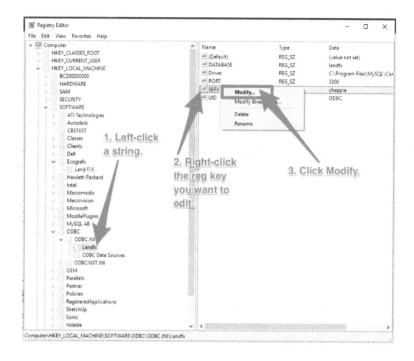

In the **Edit String** dialog box, make your desired change in the **Value data** field. Click **OK** to save your change.

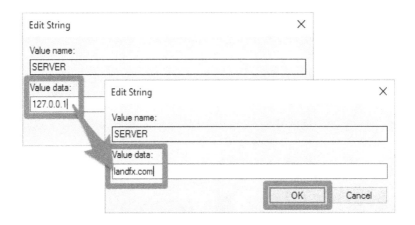

Delete a Reg Key or String Value

Before deleting a Reg Key or string value, it's a good idea to back it up by exporting it. In this example, we'll show you how to export and delete the Reg Key named **HKEY_LOCAL_MACHINE\SOFTWARE\Classes\Installer\Products\AutoCAD 2015.**

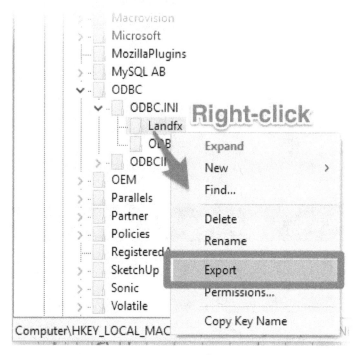

Right-click the Reg Key folder, and select **Export** from the menu that opens.

Navigate to the location where you want to back up the Reg Key, and click **Save**.

You'll now have a backed-up copy of the Reg Key, should you need it.

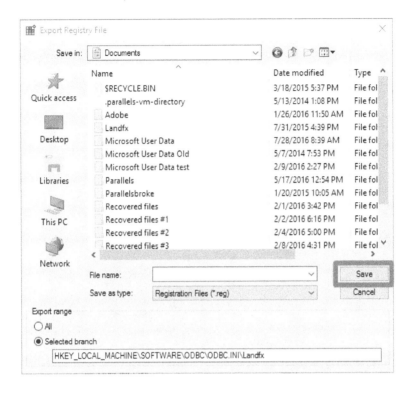

You can now delete the Reg Key safely.

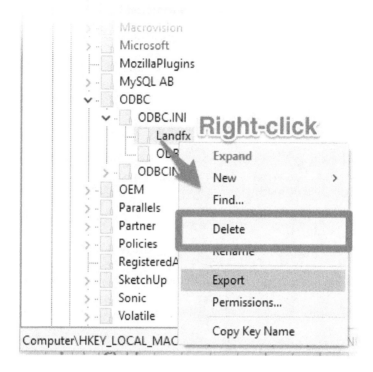

To delete the Reg Key, *right-click* it and select **Delete** from the menu that opens.

Do not delete this particular Reg Key — or any Reg Key, for that matter — unless specifically instructed to do so. The Reg Key(s) you need to delete will depend on the issue you're experiencing with AutoCAD.

Change Permissions for Reg Keys

You may also need to change the permissions settings for reg keys. Here's how to do that:

Right-click the key whose permissions you need to change.

Select the **Permissions** option from the menu that opens.

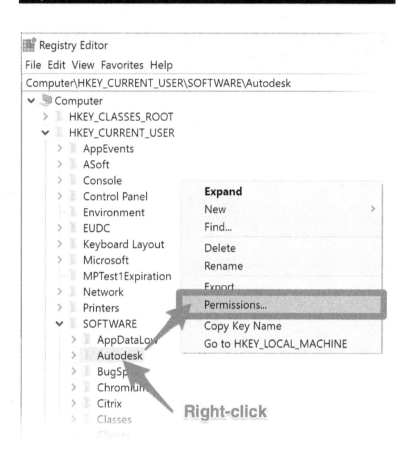

Select the user whose permissions you need to change
(example:HKEY_CURRENT_USER\SOFTWARE\ Autodesk.

Check the box for the permission type you need to grant or deny to the selected user. For example, if you need to grant the user full control (read/write access) for the key, select the **Full control** option in the **Allow** column.

Click **Apply** to apply the change, or **OK** to apply the change and close the permissions dialog box.

You'll likely need to grant permission to the **System** and **Administrator** roles as well.

You may need to restart your computer for the permission changes to take effect.

CHAPTER 3 : TROUBLESHOOTING WINDOWS REGISTRY: IDENTIFYING AND FIXING COMMON ERRORS AND ISSUES

The Windows Registry is a critical component of the Windows operating system that stores important configuration data for the system and installed software applications. However, due to its complexity and the potential for errors, it is common for users and administrators to encounter issues with the registry that can cause system instability and data loss. Here are some common errors and issues that can occur with the Windows Registry and how to troubleshoot them:

1. **Registry corruption**: Registry corruption can occur when the registry data becomes damaged or overwritten. Symptoms of registry corruption can include system crashes, blue screen errors, and other system instability issues. To troubleshoot registry corruption, you can use the System File

Checker tool to scan for and repair corrupted system files.

2. **Invalid registry entries**: Invalid registry entries can occur when a software application is improperly uninstalled or when an update or upgrade is not completed correctly. These entries can cause system errors and instability. To troubleshoot invalid registry entries, you can use a registry cleaner tool to scan and remove invalid entries.

3. **Missing registry keys or values**: Missing registry keys or values can occur when a software application is improperly installed or uninstalled. This can cause the system to be unable to access critical configuration data, leading to errors and instability. To troubleshoot missing registry keys or values, you can use the

Windows Registry Editor to manually add missing keys or values.

4. **Registry bloat**: Registry bloat can occur when the registry becomes cluttered with unused or unnecessary keys and values. This can cause system performance issues and slow boot times. To troubleshoot registry bloat, you can use a registry cleaner tool to scan and remove unused or unnecessary entries.

5. **Access permissions issues**: Access permissions issues can occur when users or applications are denied access to specific registry keys or values. This can cause software applications to fail or not function correctly. To troubleshoot access permissions issues, you can use the Windows Registry Editor to modify the permissions of specific keys or values.

Here's how to identify, isolate, and fix registry problems—and when to just not bother at all.

What Is the Windows Registry?

The <u>Windows Registry is essentially a massive internal database</u> containing important, machine-specific information regarding almost everything in your machine:

> System Hardware

> Installed Software and Drivers

> System Settings

> Profile Information

Opening a program, installing new software, and altering your hardware all require Windows to refer to the information contained in the registry. It's no wonder that when things start to go wrong, 'experts' decide to meddle with the registry without understanding the implications.

In reality, fragments of deleted software registries or orphaned registries are minuscule in size and shouldn't cause your machine any problems at all.

However, when the time comes to fix a real problem with your registry, it is important to know what you are doing, and the best way is often the easiest.

What Causes a Registry Error?

There are several common causes of registry errors, some worth worrying about, others not:

1. **Orphaned Entries:** Not an issue. Orphaned entries occur when you uninstall programs, and small fragments

of registry entries are left behind. Many registry fix software will proclaim these are an immediate issue, but in reality, they amount to nothing more than a few kilobytes of data in your machine.

2. **Duplicate Keys**: Not an issue. Duplicate keys are made when you reinstall, upgrade, or update software on your machine, including the operating system. Registry fix software will advise that your software will be 'confused' by the duplicate entries, slowing your machine, but in reality, this is unlikely.

3. **Fragmented Registry**: Not an issue. Similar to duplicate keys, the registry fragments when software is uninstalled, upgraded, or updated.

4. **System Shutdown Errors**: Unlikely to cause issues. Each time your computer shuts down, a copy of the registry is

saved to the system memory. If your computer is suddenly turned off, or crashes, or dies for another reason, it *could cause* an issue in the future—but this is unlikely.

5. **Malware and Viruses**: Massive issue. Malware and viruses of all types regularly attack and modify the registry and will require immediate attention.

Registry cleaner software will commonly identify issues 1–4 as seriously important, device destroying issues. Realistically, only issue 5 should cause you to take immediate action.

Windows is a complicated beast. Its timeless interface underpinned by countless processing at any one moment, strange "services" that you had no idea existed until you stumbled upon them that one time in task manager, and registry keys — virtually tons of registry keys.

The registry is a massive database in Windows that contains special binary keys that relate to all the installed applications and settings on your machine. If a registry error occurs, it may stop its associated app from functioning properly or even blue-screen your PC. Here's our guide on how to deal with registry errors.

Why Do Registry Errors Occur?

Even your trusty Windows PC isn't perfect (as any zealous Linux user will regularly remind you), and amid its millions of processes, things are bound to go a little wrong. Registry errors can occur when you've uninstalled programs, but some of their information stays in the registry. It could also occur when you have duplicate registry keys, don't shut down your computer correctly, or, most severely, it could be because of a virus (stressing the importance of having anti-malware protection).

How to Create a Windows Registry Backup

You should only fix and repair the Windows Registry when necessary. If you have ever encountered a particularly irksome piece of malware or virus, you will know the extreme lengths some of these infections go to disguising their activity on your machine.

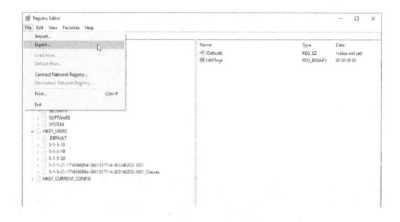

First of all, before attempting to alter, fix, or delete registry fields, you should **always** back up the Windows Registry to a secure location.

1. Input **regedit** in the Start Menu search box, and select the Best Match
2. Head to **File > Export**
3. In the dialogue box, enter a useful name such as **regbackup**, select a useful location—Documents is the default—and click **Save**

You should also note that the time to back up the Windows Registry is when you have a clean computer. If you try to create a backup when you suspect there is malware on your system, you'll back up the malicious entries, too.

How to Restore a Windows Registry Backup

Once you have a Windows Registry backup, you need to know how to restore it. There are several ways you can restore a Windows Registry backup, depending on the status of the machine.

1. Basic Windows Registry Restore

The basic method works when your computer is healthy or in a low-level state of repair.

1. Input **regedit** in the Start Menu search box, and select the Best Match
2. Head to **File > Import**
3. Browse to the location of your Windows Registry backup and select **Open**

Barring any outrageous, unaccountable errors to your system, you should now be able to back up and restore the Windows Registry.

Another, slightly quicker method for registry restoration is to simply browse to the backup location, **right-click** the registry file, and select **merge**. The .REG file will be automatically imported to your registry.

2. Restore the Registry from Safe Mode

If the Windows Registry does not restore from your standard Windows account, you can boot into Windows Safe Mode and try again.

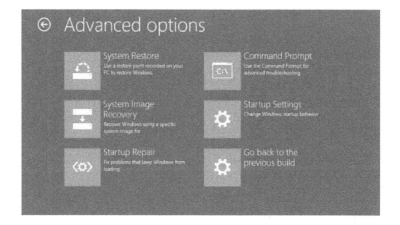

1. Type **advanced start-up** in your Start Menu search bar and select the Best Match. Now, under **Advanced start-up**, select **Restart Now**. Clicking Restart Now will restart your system in recovery mode, where you will encounter three options: **Continue**, **Troubleshoot**, or **Turn Off Your PC**.

2. Select **Troubleshoot > Advanced Options**. You now have a new range of options to choose from.

3. Select **Start-up Settings > Restart**. Your system will restart. The Start-up Settings screen will load after you reboot. From here, choose the requisite option for Safe Mode.

From here, you can follow the steps in the first section to restore your Windows Registry.

Use System Restore to Fix the Windows Registry

Before using more advanced Windows Registry restore options, such as via the Command Prompt, you can attempt to use a system restore point. Microsoft advocates using a system restore point rather than a manual Windows Registry restoration, simply because using a system restore point is much easier.

Windows will set automatic system restore points so long as the feature is switched on— or something else hasn't switched it off.

1. Press **Windows key + S** and search for **restore**.
2. Select the **create a restore point** result.
3. This will open **System Properties > System Protection,** where you can check whether protection is on, configure settings, and create a restore point right now.
4. If you want to use a system restore point, select **System Restore** and the restore point you want to use. Then follow the instructions.

One nice Windows System Restore feature is the ability to **Scan for affected programs.** If you select your system restore point, scan to see a list of the programs the system restore point will affect or delete.

Malware and viruses can disable System Restore and delete restore points. Moreover, your own anti-virus may resist any attempts to copy or modify core Windows settings, negating the effects of System Restore. However, as shown above, your system should automatically set a system restore point at each critical Windows Update.

Nonetheless, check that you have this feature turned on and create a fresh restore point for your peace of mind.

Manually Restore the Windows Registry

You can manually restore the Windows Registry using the Command Prompt. On some occasions, Windows will not boot into Safe Mode, or other issues stop the restoration of the Windows Registry. In those cases, you can use the manual restore option.

This process is a little more complex than the previous sections. Unfortunately, it also requires a little prior planning.

Since **Windows 10 version 1803**, there is no automatic Windows Registry backup. Prior to 1803, Windows would take a Registry backup every 10-days via the RegIdleBackup service.

Microsoft stopped the automatic backup to reduce the size of Windows 10 footprint with devices lacking removable storage options in mind. Also, Microsoft recommends using a system restore point to repair a corrupt registry.

Learning how to use system restore is invaluable. Here's <u>how to use a factory reset or a system restore point to fix</u> your Windows 10 machine.

Switch Automatic Registry Backups On

Reinstating automatic Windows Registry backups is a simple process involving a registry tweak.

First, Input **regedit** in the Start Menu search bar, and select the Best Match. Then, press **CTRL + F**, then copy and paste the following:

HKEY_LOCAL_MACHINE\SYSTEM\CurrentCon trolSet\Control\Session Manager\Configuration Manager

Right-click in the right panel and select **New > DWORD (32-Bit) Value**. Change the name to **EnablePeriodicBackup**. Then double-click the DWORD and change the value to **1**. Press OK. You'll have to restart your system for the change to take place.

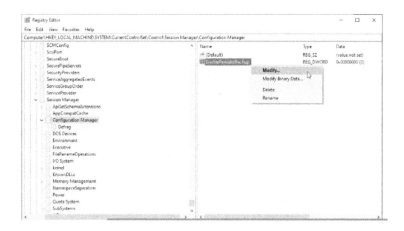

1. Enter Advanced Startup Options

If you do have an automatic backup, you can attempt to restore the registry manually. First, you need to boot into the advanced start-up options.

1. Head to **Settings > Update & Security > Recovery**
2. Select **Restart Now**

Alternatively, open your **Start Menu**, then hold the **Shift** key and press **Restart**.

Once the menu options, press **Troubleshoot > Advanced Options > Command Prompt**

2. Change the Directory

When the Command Prompt opens, it will default to **X:\Windows\System32**. This isn't the actual location of your Windows installation, so we need to move to the correct drive letter before proceeding.

By and large, your Windows installation is found on the C:\ drive, unless you move it somewhere else. However, recovery mode tends to boot your Windows installation under a different drive letter, usually D:\. To find the correct drive, input the following:

```
dir D:\Win*
```

The Command Prompt will list the directory contents, so you'll know it is the correct drive.

Now, enter the following commands, in order:

```
cd d:\windows\system32\config
```

```
xcopy *.* C:\RegBack\
```

cd RegBack

dir

Check the dates of the files in the RegBack directory. If they are from before your issue began, you can enter the following commands:

copy /y software ..

copy /y system ..

copy /y sam ..

And yes, the two periods are part of the command.

Following this, reboot your computer normally.

Use a Windows PE Recovery Disc

If you cannot enter the Windows recovery mode, Safe Mode, or otherwise, there is a final option. You can use a Windows PE recovery drive to attempt to fix or restore your Windows Registry.

A Windows PE recovery CD or USB is a Windows environment that you boot from the disc or USB, before your operating system loads. Booting from a USB allows you to fix issues with the host machine, especially handy if the host has malware or other issues.

There are several bootable Windows PE-based recovery discs available. Once you boot into the Windows PE environment, you can attempt to restore the Windows Registry using one of the previous methods.

When Not to Bother Fixing Windows Registry Errors

So, when should you not bother fixing the Windows Registry? The answer is that most of the time, you should steer clear of the registry unless you know what you're doing, or a technician advises you to make specific edits.

Some malware removal guides will advise you to remove specific registry entries. In some cases, they are right. But in many cases purported quick registry fixes to speed your computer are almost always snake oil solutions.

Not every person who advises registry fixes is a charlatan, and those that know what they are doing can eek a little more performance out of your device. Plus, several nice little tweaks can alter Windows appearance: removing the irritating shortcut symbol for is one example.

But as we said, as soon as you dive into the registry, **make a backup!**

What Happens If I Delete the Entire Registry?

Thankfully, Windows is full of fail-safes.

Unless you really try and also understand how to execute advanced commands, you cannot just CTRL+A, DELETE your entire registry. That would cause your system to implode, bringing the very fabric of the universe down with it.

Seriously though, Windows doesn't want you to delete the entire registry, because your computer will not work.

Only Repair the Windows 10 Registry When You Have To

Errors, corruption, issues, viruses, ransomware, scamware, and malware do happen. Protect yourself and the Windows Registry by:

> ➢ Making a system restore point
> ➢ Taking a system image
> ➢ Making a registry backup

And save them all to external drives for extra protection!

Disabling the Registry Editor (Policy Plus)

This method is for Windows 10 Home users only.

Windows 10 Home does not include the Local Group Policy Editor. But if you're using Windows 10 Home, you can use the free, portable, open source program Policy Plus instead.

If you're using Windows 10 Pro or Enterprise, you have access to the Local Group Policy Editor. You don't need to use Policy Plus. In fact, you shouldn't. The Local Group Policy Editor overrides Policy Plus. So it doesn't make sense to use Policy Plus if you already have the Local Group Policy Editor.

To use Policy Plus, <u>download the EXE file</u> and run it. No installation is needed.

Not all templates are included in Policy Plus by default. To download the latest policy files and add them to Policy Plus, go to **Help > Acquire ADMX Files**.

Accept the default **Destination folder** and click **Begin**.

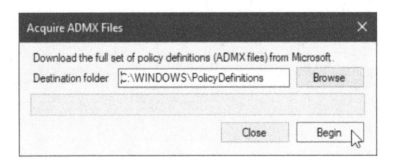

Click **Yes** to open and load the ADMX files in Policy Plus.

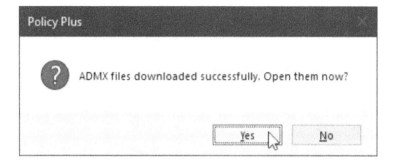

To disable access to the Registry Editor using Policy Plus, select **System** in the left pane. Then, double-click the **Prevent access to registry editing tools** setting in the left pane.

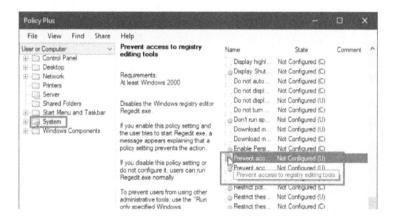

On the **Edit Policy Setting** dialog box, select **Enabled** and click **OK**.

You may have to change this setting and reboot a few times for it to take effect.

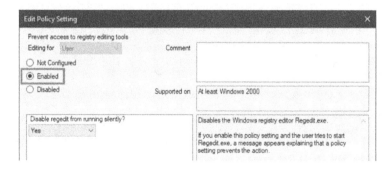

Policy Plus also allows you to search for settings by unique ID, registry (search by key path or name or value name), and text (find in title, descriptions, and in comments).

That's it! Now the registry editor should be restricted for the user account. Of course, this isn't the only way to reduce privileges on Windows.

How Do I Detect Registry Errors?

Registry errors can manifest in strange ways, such as by blue-screen crashes or by cryptic error messages occurring when your computer starts up. Sometimes things are a little more obvious, and you'll get an explicit message when your PC crashes that a registry error has occurred, or upon startup Windows

Registry Checker may tell you that "Windows registry is damaged."

While the latter problem may be down to defective hardware, registry errors can usually be fixed using several processes on Windows.

Preparation for Fixing Registry Errors

First up, create a system restore point by going to "Control Panel -> System -> Advanced System Settings," then clicking the "System Protection" tab and selecting "Create."

Next, you'll want to back up your registry. Press "Win + R", then in the Run box type **regedit** and hit Enter.

In the Registry Editor scroll all the way to the top in the left-hand pane, right-click "Computer" and click "Export."

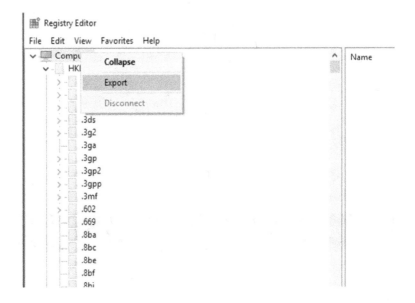

Give the backup file a name you'll remember, and save it in a safe place (cloud storage or a flash drive is a good idea).

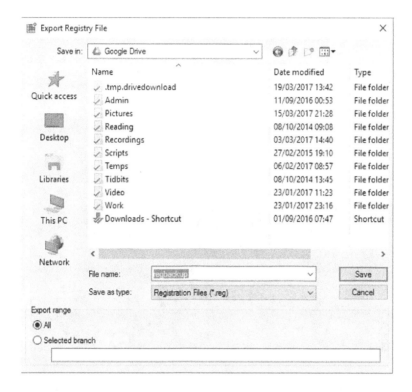

How to Fix Your Registry

The first port of call is the System File Checker. To use it, open the command prompt as an administrator, then type sfc /scannow and hit Enter. This will check your drive for registry errors and replace any registries it deems faulty.

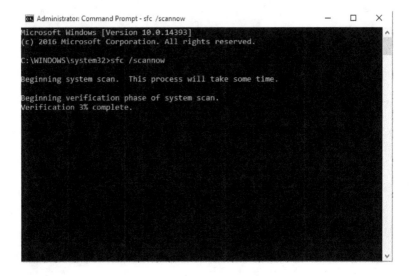

If you're having problems with a particular piece of software, reinstalling it doesn't seem to help (or indeed, the problems started since reinstalling), and if the above method doesn't work, I recommend using CCleaner to do the job. This reputable app is a great all-round system cleaner and has a dedicated tool for finding and fixing registry errors.

*O*nce you've installed CCleaner, just click

Registry on the left-hand side, then "Scan for

Issues." Once it's discovered all the problems

(there will always be some), scroll through the

list to see if there's one relating to the

program that's causing you trouble. Either

way, you may as well fix all the issues it's

discovered, so make sure they're all selected

and click "Fix selected issues."

Chapter 4 : Optimizing Windows Registry: Maximizing System Performance and Speed

The Windows Registry is a critical component of the Windows operating system. It stores configuration settings for the operating system, installed applications, and user preferences. Over time, the Registry can become cluttered with unused or outdated entries, which can slow down the performance of your computer. In this book, we will explore how to optimize the Windows Registry to improve the performance of your system.

The first section of the book will introduce you to the Windows Registry and its structure. You will learn about the different types of Registry keys and values, and how to navigate the Registry using the Registry Editor.

Next, we will discuss the common causes of Registry bloat and how to identify and remove unnecessary entries. You will learn how to use built-in tools such as Disk Cleanup and Registry Cleaner to clean up the Registry and improve performance.

We will also cover more advanced techniques for optimizing the Registry, such as disabling unnecessary startup programs, optimizing system settings, and optimizing the paging file.

Finally, we will explore best practices for maintaining a healthy Registry over time, including creating regular backups and using a Registry monitoring tool.

Whether you are an IT professional responsible for managing a fleet of Windows computers or a home user looking to improve the performance of your personal computer, this book will provide you with the knowledge and skills necessary to optimize the Windows Registry and keep your system running smoothly.

Methods To Optimize Windows 10 Performance

Method 1: Restart Device

The first and foremost step to boost your system is to restart it as it fixes most of the fundamental issues on your system. Also, restarting the system makes it easier to optimize Windows 10.

Follow the steps listed below to restart your system:

#1) Click on the Windows button and then click on the "Power" button. Finally, click on "Restart" as shown in the image below.

Method 2: Disable Startup Apps

The startup apps are the applications that are launched when the system starts. These programs get loaded into the memory as the system restarts. Startup apps are the most commonly used apps or antivirus software and disabling the startup applications can optimize Windows 10.

Follow these steps:

#1) Click on the search bar and search for "Startup". Click on "Startup Apps" as shown in the image below.

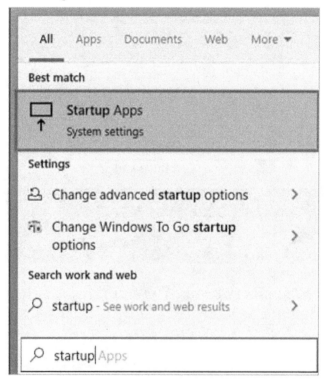

#2) A window will open. Toggle the switch to disable the application to load on the startup. Now, disable all the startup applications.

Method 3: Update Drivers

Drivers are the programs that allow the devices to sync with the system and function smoothly. Therefore, keep the drivers updated to enable the system to work in the best possible condition.

Follow the steps listed below to update the drivers:

#1) Right-click on the Windows icon and further click on "Device Manager" as shown in the image below.

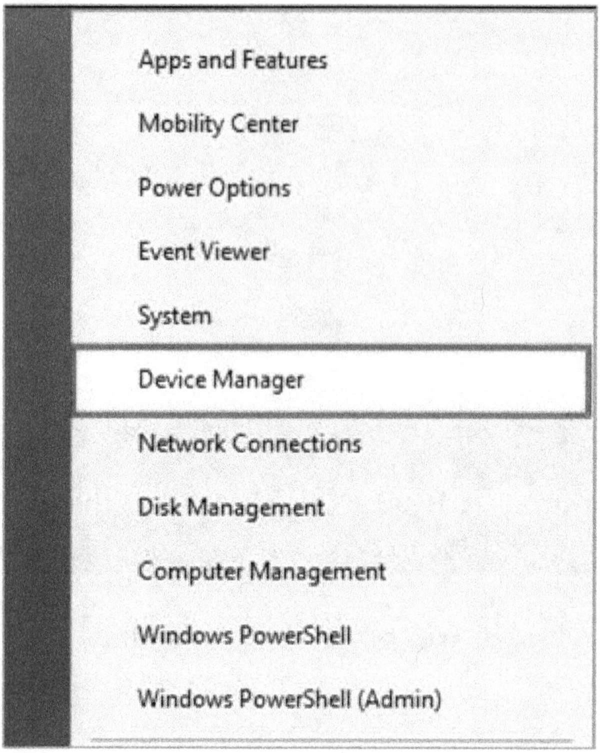

Apps and Features

Mobility Center

Power Options

Event Viewer

System

Device Manager

Network Connections

Disk Management

Computer Management

Windows PowerShell

Windows PowerShell (Admin)

#2) Right-click on all drivers and click on "Update Driver".

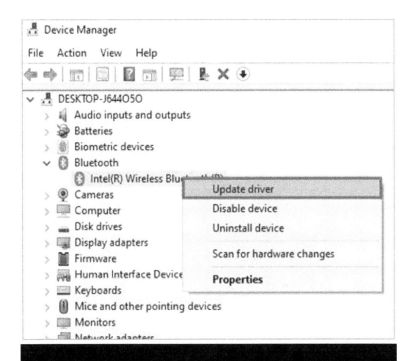

Method 4: Disable Background App

Various applications run in the background and there are a series of processes and programs that become active when these applications run in the background. This cover-up the broader section of the CPU, so you must disable background apps to optimize Windows 10.

Follow these steps to disable background app:

#1) Click on the Windows button and click on "Settings".

#2) A window will open as shown in the image below. Now, click on "Privacy".

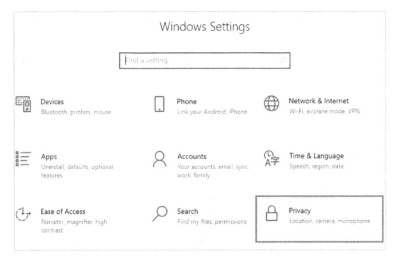

#3) Click on "Background apps", toggle the switch off under the heading "Let apps run in the background".

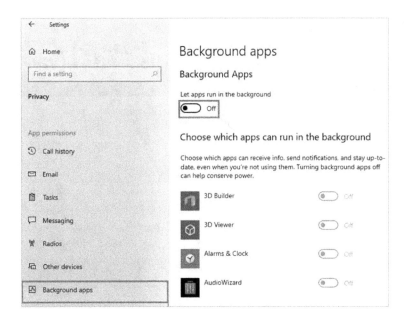

Method 5: Clean Up Hard Drive Space

When you search for any file on the hard drive, the system goes through all the files, and on finding it, comes up with the required file. This is called the dump search process. It takes a lot of time, so it is most favorable to save only critical files on the system. Other files should be uploaded on cloud storage or held on local devices, as this can optimize Windows 10.

Method 6: Use Drive Defragmentation

Whenever you delete any file or program, its place is marked as blank in the memory, but the slot for the program or file is present in the drive. Therefore, defragmentation is the process that allows you to clear these empty memory slots and allows you to utilize the entire memory.

Method 7: Configure Ready Boost

Windows provides its users with the features to store the cache files in the remote storage files known as Ready Boost. **Follow the steps listed below to enable Ready Boost and optimize Windows 10:**

#1) Insert flash drive in the system. Right-click on the flash drive, and click on "Properties".

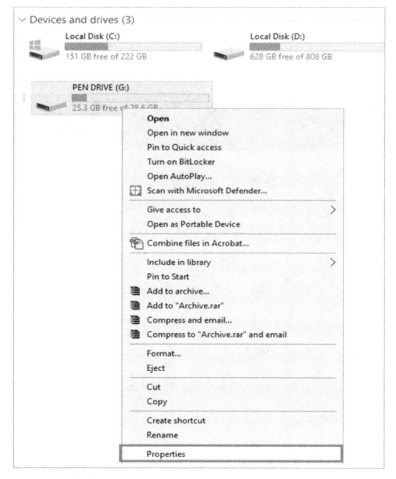

#2) A dialog box will open, as shown in the image below. Now, click on "ReadyBoost" and select the option "Dedicate this device to ReadyBoost". Click on apply, then click on "OK".

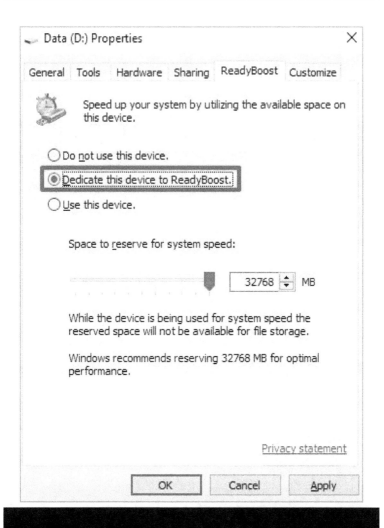

Method 8: Perform Malware Scan

The malicious and infected files remain the most crucial reason responsible for the slowing down of the system, so it is essential to <u>perform malware scans</u> on your system to keep your system in good condition and to optimize Windows 10.

Method 9: Install Latest Updates

Windows works on the issues and feedbacks submitted by its users, and therefore it works on fixing these issues and making Windows faster. Windows releases the latest updates for its users, so you must install the latest updates on your system to achieve the best output from it.

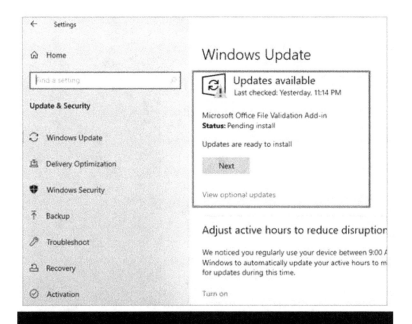

Method 10: Switch To High-Performance Power Plan

The power settings in Windows allow users to make choices between the power usage plans and these plans offer either long battery life or high performance. You can make the choices based on your requirements. By **choosing the high performance, you can** <u>**optimize Windows 10**</u>.

Follow these steps:

#1) Click on start and then click on "Settings" as shown in the image below.

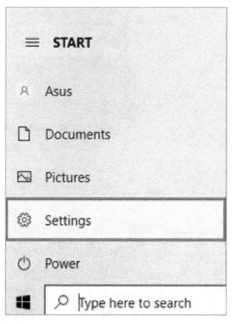

#2) A window will open, as shown in the image below. Click on "System".

#3) Click on "Power & sleep" as shown in the image below, and then click on "Additional power settings".

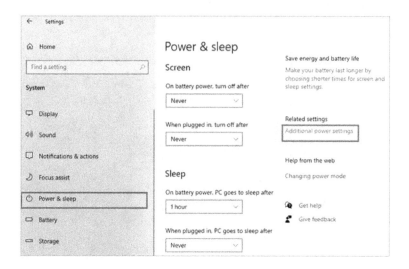

#4) Click on "Create a power plan" as shown in the image below.

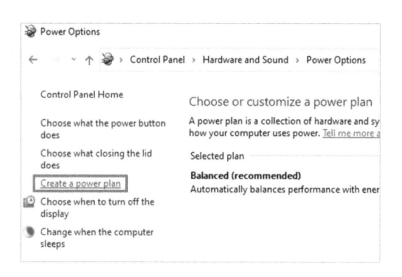

#5) Click on "High performance" and then click on "Next".

Create a Power Plan

← ∨ ↑ > Control Panel > Hardware and Sound > Power Options > Create a Power Plan

Create a power plan

Start with an existing plan and give it a name.

○ **Balanced (recommended)**
Automatically balances performance with energy consumption on capable hardware.

○ Power saver
Saves energy by reducing your computer's performance where possible.

⦿ High performance
Favors performance, but may use more energy.

Plan name:
My Custom Plan 1

[Next]   [Cancel]

Method 11: Disable System Visual Effects

Disabling the special visual effects on the graphical interface can make it easier for the system to function smoothly. It can also make it easier to optimize Windows 10.

Follow the steps listed below to disable system visual effects:

#1) Open Settings, System, and then click on About. Now, click on "Advanced system settings," as shown in the image below.

Related settings

BitLocker settings

Device Manager

Remote desktop

System protection

Advanced system settings

Rename this PC (advanced)

 Get help

Give feedback

#2) As shown in the image below, a dialog box will open, click on "Advanced". Then, under the heading performance, click on "Settings".

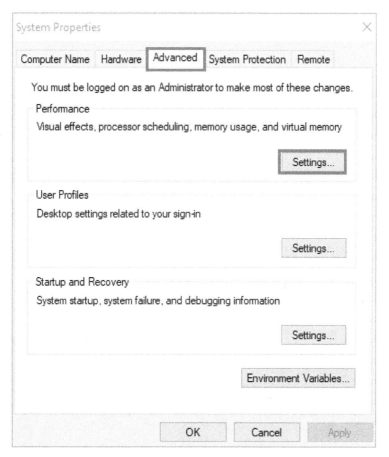

#3) A dialog box will open, click on "Visual Effects" and then click on the title "Adjust for

best performance". Click on "Apply" and
"OK".

| Visual Effects | Advanced | Data Execution Prevention |

Select the settings you want to use for the appearance and
performance of Windows on this computer.

○ Let Windows choose what's best for my computer

○ Adjust for best appearance

◉ Adjust for best performance

○ Custom:

- [ ] Animate controls and elements inside windows
- [ ] Animate windows when minimizing and maximizing
- [ ] Animations in the taskbar
- [ ] Enable Peek
- [ ] Fade or slide menus into view
- [ ] Fade or slide ToolTips into view
- [ ] Fade out menu items after clicking
- [ ] Save taskbar thumbnail previews
- [ ] Show shadows under mouse pointer
- [ ] Show shadows under windows
- [ ] Show thumbnails instead of icons
- [ ] Show translucent selection rectangle
- [ ] Show window contents while dragging
- [ ] Slide open combo boxes
- [ ] Smooth edges of screen fonts
- [ ] Smooth-scroll list boxes
- [ ] Use drop shadows for icon labels on the desktop

| OK | Cancel | Apply |

Method 12: Disable Search Indexing

Whenever you search for anything on the system, all the folders arrange their folders and subfolders as indexes that cover a more significant part of the CPU. So by enabling this search indexing, Windows can be made to perform faster.

Follow the steps listed below to disable search indexing and optimize Windows 10:

#1) Open Settings, search for "Searching Windows" and a screen will appear as shown in the image below. Then click on "Advanced Search Indexer Settings."

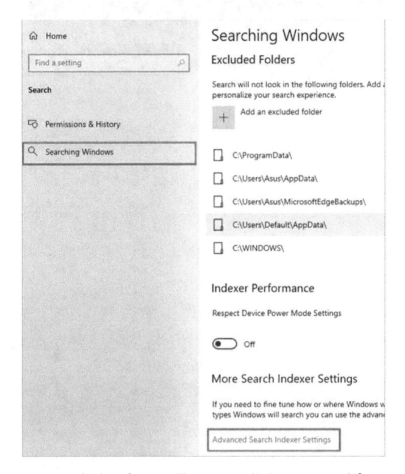

#2) A dialog box will open. Click on "Modify".

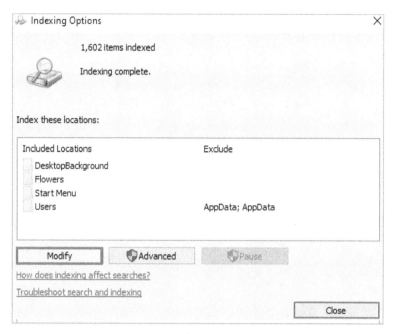

#3) Un-check all the folders and click on "OK" as shown in the image below.

Indexed Locations   ✕

Change selected locations

☐   csc://{S-1-5-21-2633412029-1173096131-810271229-1001}
☐   dp://{S-1-5-21-2633412029-1173096131-810271229-1001}/
☐ > Local Disk (C:)
☐ > Local Disk (D:)
☐ > PEN DRIVE (G:)

‹   ›

Summary of selected locations

Included Locations	Exclude
DesktopBackground	
Flowers	
Start Menu	
Users	AppData; AppData

Show all locations   OK   Cancel

Method 13: Increase Page File Size

Windows restricts the memory usage for each application, and by increasing that memory usage, you can increase the system's speed, and hence you can optimize Windows 10.

Follow the steps listed below to increase page file size:

#1) Open Settings, click on System and then click on About. Now, click on "Advanced system settings" as shown below.

This page has a few new settings

Some settings from Control Panel
have moved here, and you can copy
your PC info so it's easier to share.

Related settings

BitLocker settings

Device Manager

Remote desktop

System protection

Advanced system settings

Rename this PC (advanced)

Get help

Give feedback

#2) A dialog box will open. Now, click on
"Advanced" and then click on "Settings"
under the Performance title.

System Properties   ✕

Computer Name   Hardware   Advanced   System Protection   Remote

You must be logged on as an Administrator to make most of these changes.

Performance

Visual effects, processor scheduling, memory usage, and virtual memory

Settings...

User Profiles

Desktop settings related to your sign-in

Settings...

Startup and Recovery

System startup, system failure, and debugging information

Settings...

Environment Variables...

OK   Cancel   Apply

#3) Click on "Change".

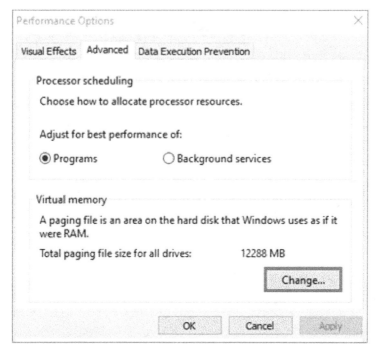

#4) Uncheck "Automatically manage paging file size for all drives" as shown in the image below, and then click on "Custom size" enter specified values and then click on "Set" and finally on "OK."

Virtual Memory   ×

☐ Automatically manage paging file size for all drives

Paging file size for each drive

Drive [Volume Label]   Paging File Size (MB)

C:	System managed
D:	None

Selected drive: C:
Space available: 167636 MB

◉ Custom size:

Initial size (MB):   [   ]

Maximum size (MB):   [   ]

○ System managed size

○ No paging file   [Set]

Total paging file size for all drives

Minimum allowed: 16 MB

Recommended: 1393 MB

Currently allocated: 12288 MB

[OK]   [Cancel]

Method 14: Restore Previous Working State

If your system starts working slowly, then it is best to switch to the previous system version. So you can perform System Restore to restore the system to the last working point.

Method 15: Repair Windows Setup Files

Windows provides its users with the feature to Restore system health and fix Windows setup files using the command line. **Follow the steps listed below to optimize Windows 10 by repairing Windows setup files:**

#1) Click on the Windows button and search for Command Prompt and click on "Run as administrator".

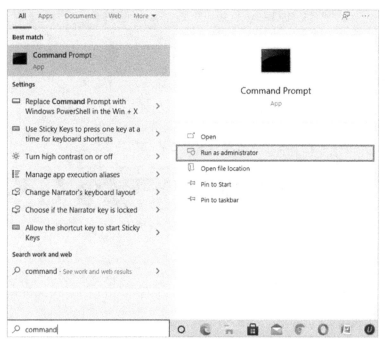

#2) Type "DISM/Online / Cleanup-image /Restorehealth" and press Enter.

```
C:\WINDOWS\system32>DISM /Online /Cleanup-image /Restorehealth

Deployment Image Servicing and Management tool
Version: 10.0.19041.844

Image Version: 10.0.19043.1083

[ =====================            37.7%                        ]
```

Method 16: Reset Device To Factory Defaults

If your system is working slowly, you can also reset the entire system, and it will not affect any of the files on the hard disk, but it will reset all the settings and configurations to their default mode.

Follow the steps listed below to **reset the device to factory default** and for optimizing Windows:

#1) Press the Windows button and click on "Settings".

#2) Click on "Update & security".

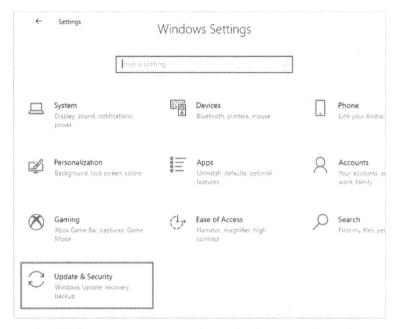

#3) Click on "Recovery" and then under the heading Reset this PC. Click on "Get started" as shown in the image below.

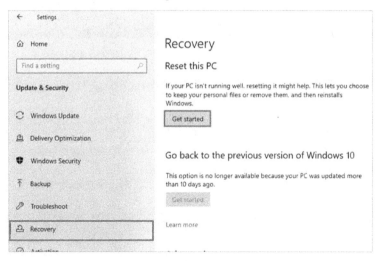

Method 17: Upgrade To Faster Drive

The main factor and the hardware device on which the system's speed depends is the boot device. Use SSD as your boot device because SSD is much faster than HDDs and thus allows the system to function efficiently. It is best suited to switch to SSDs for Windows 10 optimization.

Method 18: Upgrade System Memory

The more memory in the system allows the user to make various partitions and store files on multiple partitions, which narrows down the search for the crawler. So you must add more memory to your system or should even use a storage device to store data in it and connect it to the system when that data is needed.

This is an efficient way to optimize Windows 10 performance settings.

Method 19: Run Troubleshooters

Windows provides its users with various types of troubleshooters, making it easier for them to troubleshoot multiple devices and hence fix the issues with the devices.

Follow the steps listed below to locate and fix various issues using troubleshooters and optimizing Windows 10:

#1) Press the Windows button and click on "Settings" as shown in the image below.

#2) Click on "Update & security".

#3) Click on "Troubleshoot" and further click on "Additional troubleshooters" as shown in the image below.

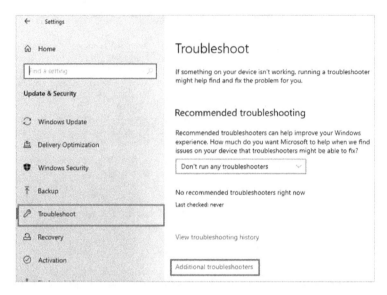

#4) A list of troubleshooters will appear.

⌂ Additional troubleshooters

Get up and running

Internet Connections
Find and fix problems with connecting to the Internet or to websites.

Playing Audio
Find and fix problems with playing sound

Printer
Find and fix problems with printing

Windows Update
Resolve problems that prevent you from updating Windows.

Find and fix other problems

Bluetooth
Find and fix problems with Bluetooth devices

Connection to a Workplace Using DirectAccess
Find and fix problems with connecting to your workplace network using DirectAccess.

Incoming Connections
Find and fix problems with incoming computer connections and Windows Firewall.

Keyboard
Find and fix problems with your computer's keyboard settings.

Network Adapter
Find and fix problems with wireless and other network adapters.

Power
Find and fix problems with your computer's power settings to conserve power and extend battery life.

Method 20: Add More RAM

The most efficient way to increase the system's speed is by increasing the RAM of the system, so add more RAM to the device and optimize Windows 10.

Method 21: Adjust Appearance

Various personalization settings take a share of the RAM and utilize the more significant amount of power supply.

Follow the tips listed below which can make it easier for you to optimize Windows 10:

1. Switch to dark mode.
2. Reduce the brightness of the screen.
3. Put up dark wallpaper, so it does not utilize too much power.

4. Do not connect too many devices to the system.

5. Keep Wi-Fi and Bluetooth turned off when not in use.

6. Keep track of the Task Manager and the CPU Usage.

Method 22: Manage Power Settings

The power settings allow the users to manage the working of the system. Also, it will enable you to choose the power plan, so follow the steps listed below to control the power settings and optimize Windows 10:

#1) Click on start and then click on "Settings".

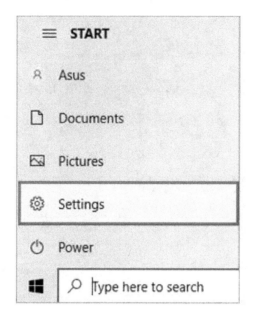

#2) A window will open, as shown in the image below, then click on "System".

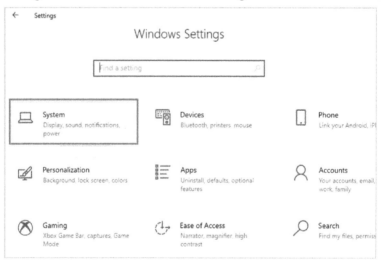

#3) Click on "Power & sleep". Then click on "Additional power settings".

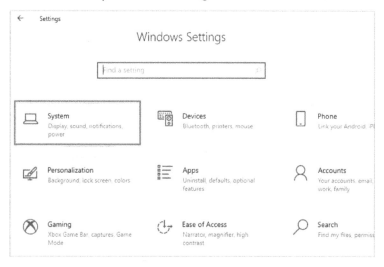

#4) Click on "Create a power plan" as shown below.

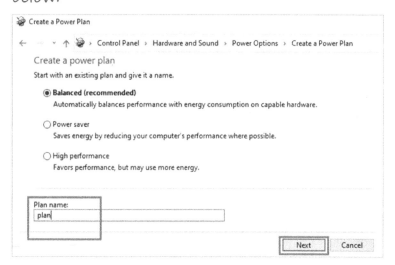

#5) *Customize the plan according to the requirement and click on "Create".*

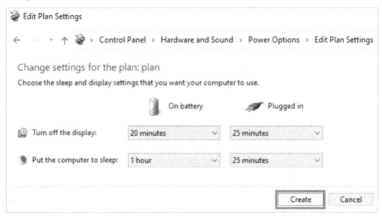

Method 23: Disable One Drive Sync

One drive is a feature from Microsoft which allows users to access cloud storage and work over the server, but One Drive sync itself with the system and runs in the background, thereby slowing down the system's speed.

Follow the step listed below to Disable One Drive sync and optimize Windows 10:

#1) Locate the One Drive icon on the taskbar, click on the icon, click on more, and then click on Pause One Drive sync.

Method 24: Shut Windows Tips and Tricks

The Widows Tips and tricks is a process that works in the background and utilizes both CPU and Internet, so you must disable Windows Tips and tricks to optimize Windows 10.

Follow the steps listed below to Disable Windows Tips and tricks:

#1) Click on start and then click on "Settings" as shown in the image below.

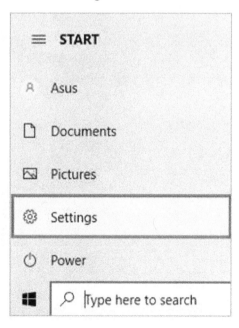

#2) A window will open. Click on "System".

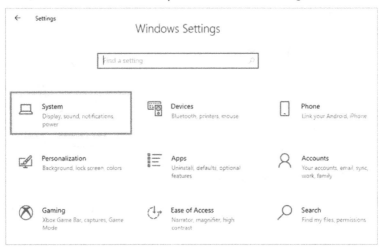

#3) Click on "Notifications & sound" as shown in the image below and uncheck all the options, and toggle "Get notifications from other apps and senders" to off.

← Settings

⌂ Home

Find a setting 🔎

System

🖵 Display

🔊 Sound

🖵 Notifications & actions

🌙 Focus assist

⏻ Power & sleep

🖵 Battery

🖴 Storage

🖵 Tablet

🖳 Multitasking

🖥 Projecting to this PC

Notifications & actions

Quick actions

You can add, remove, or rearrange your quick actions directly in act center.

Edit your quick actions

Notifications

Get notifications from apps and other senders

⬤ Off

To control times when you do or don't get notifications, try Focus a Focus assist settings

☑ Show notifications on the lock screen

☑ Show reminders and incoming VoIP calls on the lock screen

☑ Allow notifications to play sounds

☐ Show me the Windows welcome experience after updates and occasionally when I sign in to highlight what's new and sugges

☐ Suggest ways I can finish setting up my device to get the most of Windows

☐ Get tips, tricks, and suggestions as you use Windows

CHAPTER 5 : ADVANCED WINDOWS REGISTRY TECHNIQUES: CUSTOMIZING AND FINE-TUNING YOUR PC

Welcome to "Advanced Windows Registry Techniques: Customizing and Fine-tuning Your PC." In this book, we will explore advanced techniques for customizing and fine-tuning your Windows PC by leveraging the power of the Windows Registry.

The first section of the book will review the fundamentals of the Windows Registry, including its structure, key types, and values. We will also review the basics of Registry editing, including how to use the Registry Editor and create backups.

Next, we will dive into advanced Registry techniques, such as customizing the Windows interface, optimizing system performance, and improving security. You will learn how to use the Registry to tweak system settings, customize the desktop and taskbar, and add new features to Windows.

We will also cover advanced techniques for optimizing system performance, such as adjusting virtual memory settings, managing startup programs, and fine-tuning network settings. You will learn how to use the Registry to control system processes, services, and drivers, and how to optimize performance for specific applications.

Finally, we will explore Registry security, including how to secure the Registry and prevent unauthorized access. You will learn how to use the Registry to control user access, encrypt sensitive data, and audit system activity.

Whether you are an IT professional responsible for managing a fleet of Windows computers or a power user looking to get the most out of your PC, this book will provide you with the knowledge and skills necessary to customize and fine-tune your Windows PC using advanced Registry techniques. By the end of the book, you will be equipped to create a custom-tailored Windows environment that meets your specific needs and preferences.

Windows Registry Editor holds the capacity to customize your Windows experience and deal with little nuisances that Microsoft wrongly assumes every user will love. From changing the Windows design to unlocking hidden features, there are tweaks for everything. To help you make your Windows even better, here are a bunch of Windows registry hacks worth trying.

Warning: messing with the registry could corrupt your Windows. It is recommended that you follow the instructions precisely and don't mess around if you don't know what you are doing. Just to be safe, create a backup of your registry before making any changes.

Accessing Windows Registry in Windows

As all the tweaks require a trip to the Registry Editor in Windows, it is important to know how to access it.

1. Press the |Win| + |R| keys and type regedit in the "Run" dialog that pops up.

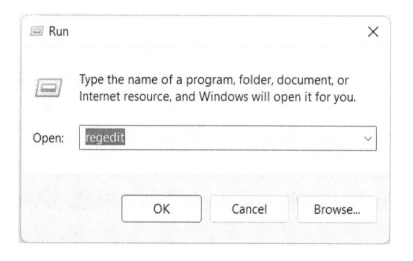

2. Click "OK" and the Windows Registry will open.

3. You can also launch it by typing regedit or "Registry Editor" in the Windows search box.

1. Add Command Prompt to Context Menu

Typing things manually into the Command Prompt all the time can be a pain. It would be much easier if, say, you could just open the Command Prompt by right-clicking on a particular location. Well, you can!

1. In the Registry Editor, navigate to:

HKEY_CLASSES_ROOT\Directory\shell\cmd

2. At this point, you'll need to <u>take ownership of the "cmd" registry key</u>, as it's protected by default. Right-click the "cmd registry-key" and select "Permissions."

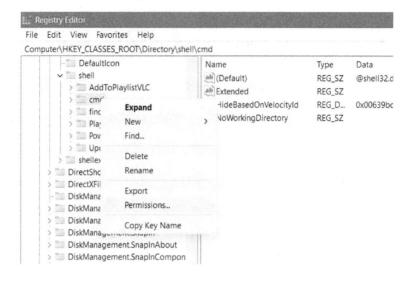

3. Click "Advanced" in the pop-up window that opens. It will lead to a new window where you can edit the registry key owner.

Permissions for cmd ✕

Security

Group or user names:

ALL APPLICATION PACKAGES
Account Unknown(S-1-15-3-1024-1065365936-1281604716-35117
SYSTEM
Administrators (DESKTOP-7GCH622\Administrators)
Users (DESKTOP-7GCH622\Users)

Add... | Remove

Permissions for ALL APPLICATION
PACKAGES | Allow | Deny

Full Control | ☐ | ☐
Read | ☑ | ☐
Special permissions | ☐ | ☐

For special permissions or advanced settings, click Advanced. | Advanced

OK | Cancel | Apply

4. Click "Change" for the Owner of the registry key. It is set as "TrustedInstaller" by default. You can change it to "Administrators" in another pop-up box.

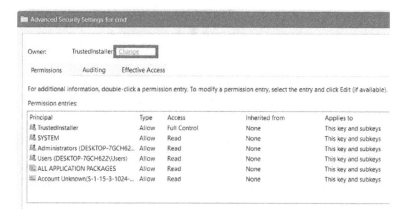

5. After approving the change, go back to
the main permission entry window
shown below. Give the admin owner
"Full control" and "Read" permissions.

6. Next, right-click the entry in the right-hand pane called "HideBasedOnVelocityId", click "Rename" and add a "_" at the start of the name so it doesn't register it anymore.

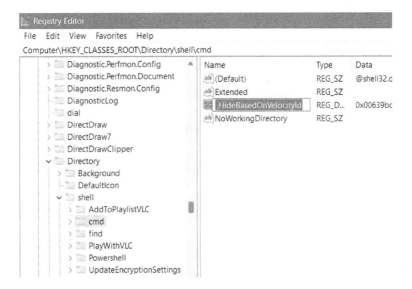

7. That's it. Close the Registry Editor and the "Open command window here" option should appear in the right-click context menu.

2. Revert to Windows 10-style Start Menu

One of the hallmark features of Windows 11 is a new-looking Start menu. It's a pretty striking look, resembling something you might see in Ubuntu or macOS, but for some, the change is a little too drastic and so they may want to go back to the old Start menu. Well, with this Windows 11 registry hack, it's possible to do so.

1. Firstly, go to Taskbar Settings by right-clicking the Taskbar at the bottom.
2. Here, ensure that the "Taskbar alignment" is left instead of the default center position.

3. Next, navigate to:

HKEY_CURRENT_USER\Software\Microsoft\Windows\CurrentVersion\Explorer\Advanced\

4. Right-click an empty space in the right-hand pane, then select "New -> DWORD 32-bit Value."

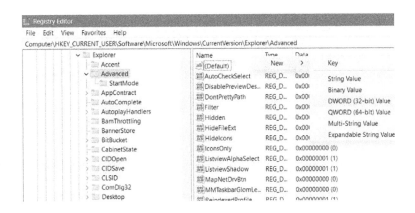

5. Name it "Start_ShowClassicMode".

6. Once it's created, double-click it and change the "Value data" to "1" to enable the Windows 10-style Start menu.

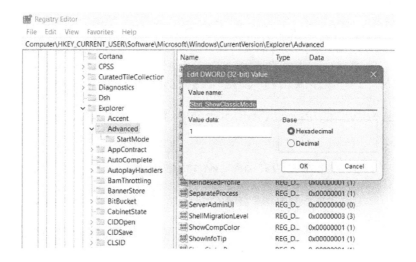

7. Restart your Windows 11 device to be greeted by the old classic Start menu.

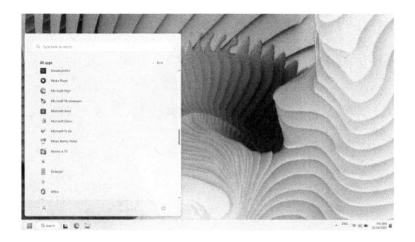

8. To switch back to the latest Start menu, change the "Taskbar alignment" to "center" and delete the "Start_ShowClassicMode" key (or set it back to the "0" value).

3. Increase Network Speeds

Many of the registry tweaks in the list involve design or aesthetic changes that may make Windows feel that much slick and better to you. But there's also a whole trove of registry hacks designed to improve your

Internet speeds. You can find them listed under locations like TCP/IP or Lanman:

Computer\HKEY_LOCAL_MACHINE\SYSTEM\ CurrentControlSet\Services\Tcpip\

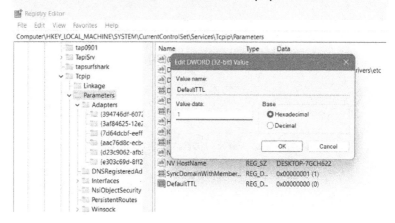

If you're having problems or experiencing packet loss, there are various things you can do, like reduce your default time to live (TTL), increase your IRP Stack Size, enable TCP extensions, or increase the maximum number of ports available to various programs trying to connect to your router.

There are enough network speed tweaks in regedit that <u>we have a whole list dedicated to it</u>. If you're mainly in the Registry Editor to improve your Internet speeds, then click on over.

4. Use Windows Photo Viewer Instead of Photos App

Everyone has, at some point, had <u>problems with the Photos app in Windows 10</u>. It's no big secret. At the same time, the Windows Photo Viewer that we know from back in the Windows 7 days did the job very well, yet it was removed with a Windows 10 update some years ago.

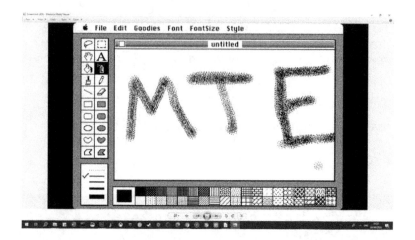

What's more, Windows Photo Viewer doesn't work in Windows 11. There's a small consolation though: the Photos app works rather flawlessly in the newer operating system.

All that being said, the code for Photo Viewer is still there in Windows 10. You just need to create a fairly elaborate registry entry to unlock it. It's a little different than your typical registry tweak, and we've created a guide for how to use the registry to <u>make</u>

<u>Windows Photo Viewer your default photo app</u> in Windows 10.

5. Disable Windows Lockscreen

The Lockscreen is a nice added layer of security on your Windows PC, requiring a password or PIN for you to log back in. If you feel like you don't need that, you can turn the Lockscreen off altogether.

1. Go down the following path and make a new key called "Personalization."

Computer\HKEY_LOCAL_MACHINE\SOFTWARE\Policies\Microsoft\Windows

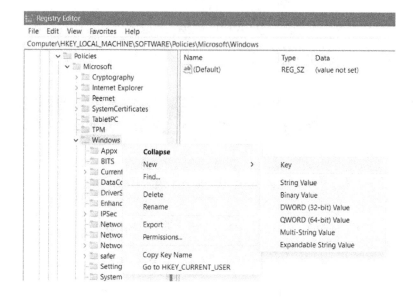

2. Create a new DWORD (32-bit value) called "NoLockScreen."

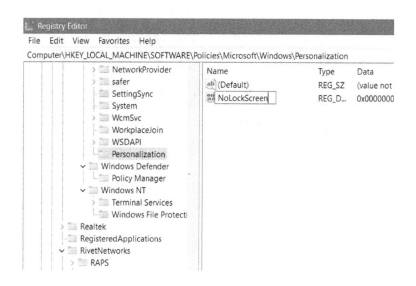

3. Double-click the newly created key to edit its value to "1" instead of the default "0."

Note: there are other ways you can do this in Windows, such as using third-party apps that disable the Lockscreen. But we wouldn't recommend that.

6. Show Detailed Information on Startup

If your PC is experiencing slowdowns or inexplicable crashes, then you should make it your priority to diagnose what's causing those problems. One possible way to do this is to set the Windows startup to "Verbose Mode," which will give you a much more detailed breakdown of the processes happening on your PC as you boot.

1. To activate this, go to the following registry key:

HKEY_LOCAL_MACHINE\SOFTWARE\Wow64 32Node\Microsoft\Windows\CurrentVersion\P olicies\System

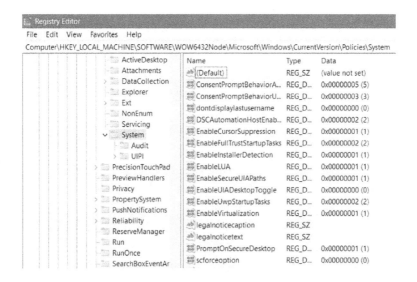

2. Right-click an empty space in the pane on the right, then select "New -> DWORD (32-bit) Value."

3. Name the value "VerboseStatus."

4. Double-click on it to change its "Value data" from "0" to "1."

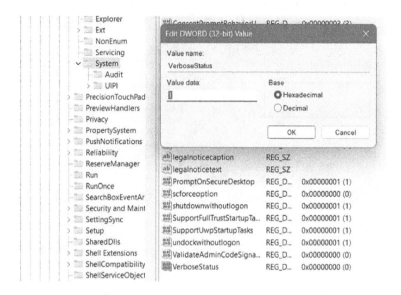

7. Open Last Active Window in Taskbar

Ever since Windows 7, open apps on the Taskbar (or Start bar) have had their own icons, with each open window or instance of that app bundled under that one icon, and visible in thumbnails when you hover your mouse over the icon. This is designed to save space in your Taskbar and generally make things neater.

By default, when you click a Taskbar icon for an open app, these thumbnails pop up, but you can make a registry tweak so that when you click a taskbar icon, the last active window of that app opens, which can save some time.

1. Go to the following path:

HKEY_CURRENT_USER\SOFTWARE\Microsoft\ Windows\CurrentVersion\Explorer\Advanced

2. On the right side of the key, create a new DWORD (32-bit) value named "LastActiveClick."

3. Double-click on it to change its value from "0" to "1."

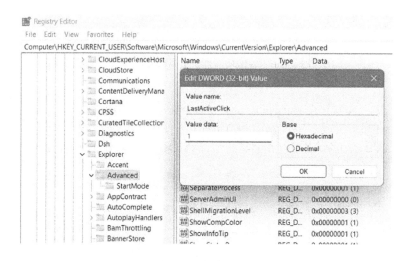

8. Disable Shake to Minimize

The "Aero Shake" is a feature introduced in Windows 7 that lets you minimize windows by grabbing the one you want to keep open and "shaking" it. While it may sound cool, the option can sometimes minimize all your windows without you necessarily wanting that. Shake to minimize can also be a problem for people prone to hand tremors due to illness or other causes. But it can be a great help to others.

1. To enable this feature, go to the following Windows Registry path.

Computer\HKEY_CURRENT_USER\Software\Microsoft\Windows\CurrentVersion\Explorer\Advanced

2. Create a new DWORD (32-bit) value called "DisallowShaking."

Cortana	StartMenuInit	REG_D...	0x0000000d (13)
CPSS	StartMigratedBrowserPin	REG_D...	0x00000001 (1)
CuratedTileCollectior	StartShownOnUpgrade	REG_D...	0x00000001 (1)
Diagnostics	StoreAppsOnTaskbar	REG_D...	0x00000001 (1)
Dsh	TaskbarAl	REG_D...	0x00000001 (1)
Explorer	TaskbarAnimations	REG_D...	0x00000001 (1)
Accent	TaskbarAutoHideInTablet...	REG_D...	0x00000000 (0)
Advanced	TaskbarDa	REG_D...	0x00000000 (0)
StartMode	TaskbarGlomLevel	REG_D...	0x00000000 (0)
AppContract	TaskbarMn	REG_D...	0x00000000 (0)
AutoComplete	TaskbarSizeMove	REG_D...	0x00000000 (0)
AutoplayHandlers	TaskbarSmallIcons	REG_D...	0x00000000 (0)
BamThrottling	TaskbarStateLastRun	REG_BI...	d9 da a5 63 00 00 00 00
BannerStore	UseCompactMode	REG_D...	0x00000001 (1)
BitBucket	WebView	REG_D...	0x00000001 (1)
CabinetState	WinXMigrationLevel	REG_D...	0x00000001 (1)
CIDOpen	DisallowShaking	REG_D...	0x00000000 (0)
CIDSave			
CLSID			

3. Change its default value from "0" to "1."

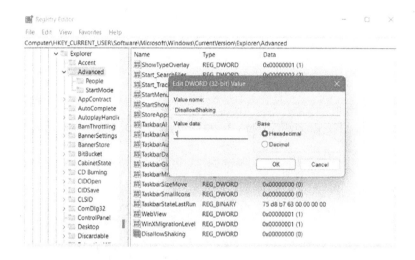

9. Add Your Own Apps and Options to the Context Menu

The context menu is a fine thing, but to really take control of it, you can create registry keys to add specific apps or Windows features to it. The exact way to do this will depend on what you want to add to the context menu. There is a nice registry hack for adding "Check for Updates" to the context menu, for example.

1. Navigate to the following path:

HKEY_CLASSES_ROOT\DesktopBackground\Shell

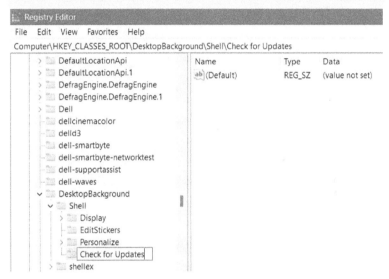

2. Right-click on the "Shell" folder and create two different keys: "Check for Updates" and "Command."

3. Next up, right-click "Check for Updates" and create a new String Value called "SettingsURI" as shown here.

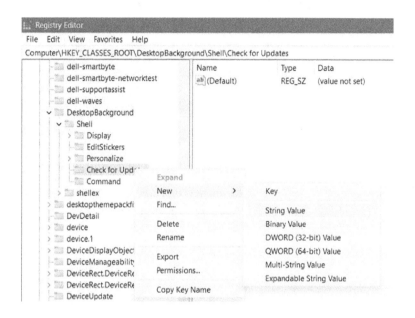

4. Double-click to reach the "Edit String" window. Enter ms-settings:windowsupdate-action in the "Value data" field

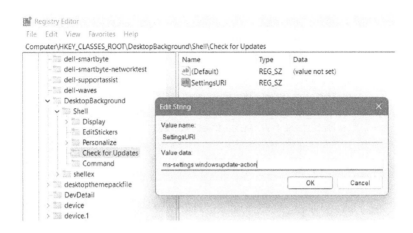

5. Repeat a similar procedure for the "Command" key with a string value "DelegateExecute" and add the value data: {556FF0D6-A1EE-49E5-9FA4-90AE116AD744}.

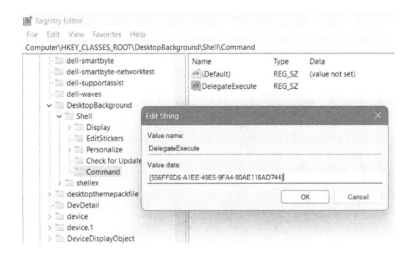

6. As soon as you create both keys with the required registry values, you should be able to see an option for checking updates within the right-click context menu.

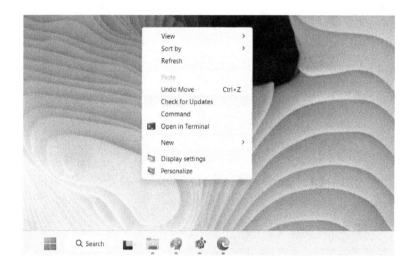

Tip: There are many other things you can do such as adding an "Open with Notepad" option to the context menu, though really you can replace Notepad in this guide with any other app on your PC.

10. Change Windows Apps and Settings to "Dark Mode"

The debate of whether reading white writing on a dark background or dark writing on a light background is healthier rages on, but if you're in the first camp, then you can use the registry to activate Dark Mode across Windows.

1. In the Windows Registry selection, go down the following path:

HKEY_CURRENT_USER\Software\Microsoft\Windows\Themes\Personalize

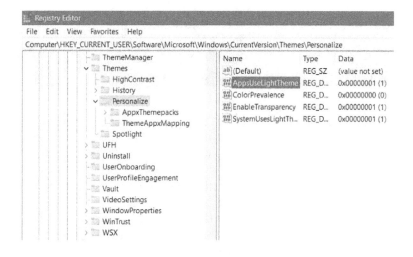

2. You should find a DWORD (32-bit) value named "AppsUseLightTheme." If it's not there, create it.

3. Change its default value from "1" to "0." All Windows apps and browsers will now assume a dark theme automatically.

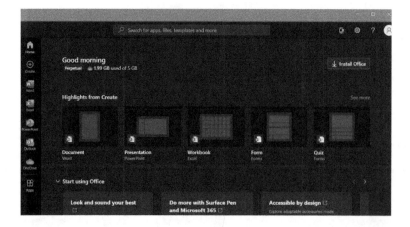

11. Remove the Windows Action Center Sidebar

The Windows Action Center Sidebar offers handy quick-access buttons and notifications. However, if you find these buttons to be unnecessary and are not comfortable with the sidebar taking up half the screen when you open it, you can simply disable it.

1. In the Registry Editor window, enter the following path:

HKEY_CURRENT_USER\Software\Policies\Microsoft\Windows\

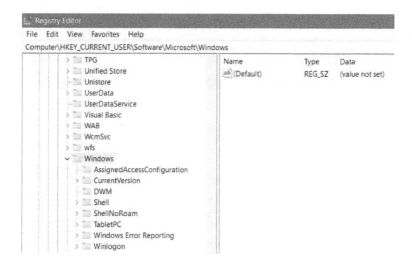

2. Create a new key under "Windows" called "Explorer" followed by a DWORD (32-bit) value for it as "DisableNotificationCenter."

3. Edit the value for the DWORD entry to "1."

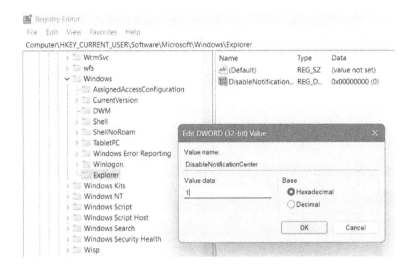

4. You won't get any new notifications in the right Action Center sidebar.

12. Remove the OneDrive Button from File Explorer

If you don't use OneDrive or shifted to another cloud storage service after Microsoft decided to downgrade its storage packages, then there is no point in having its icon in File Explorer.

1. Go to the path shown below:

HKEY_CURRENT_USER\Software\Classes\CLSI D\{018D5C66-4533-4307-9B53-224DE2ED1FE6}

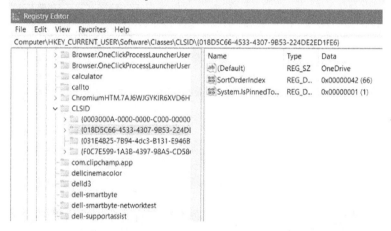

2. Change the DWORD (32-bit) value for "System.IsPinnedToNameSpaceTree" to "0" from the default "1."

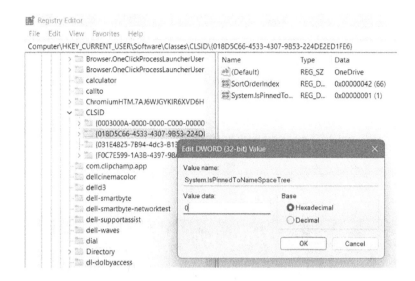

3. After that, navigate to the location below and delete the default key entry for "018D5C66-4533-4307-9B53-224DE2ED1FE6."

Computer\HKEY_CURRENT_USER\Software\Microsoft\Windows\CurrentVersion\Explorer\Desktop\NameSpace

4. OneDrive will be successfully removed upon key deletion.

13. Automatically Delete Pagefile.sys at Shutdown

The **Pagefile.sys** file is pretty handy in Windows, stepping in as virtual RAM to take some load off your physical computer RAM and help speed up the process of retrieving program data, navigating your PC quickly, and managing other vital RAM functions.

The Pagefile does, however, take up quite a bit of storage space on Windows, so here's a quick solution to automatically delete it when your PC shuts down.

1. You have to navigate to the path as shown under:

Computer\HKEY_LOCAL_MACHINE\SYSTEM\ CurrentControlSet\Control\Session Manager\Memory Management

2. Edit the DWORD (32-bit) value for "ClearPageFileAtShutdown" by changing it from "0" to "1."

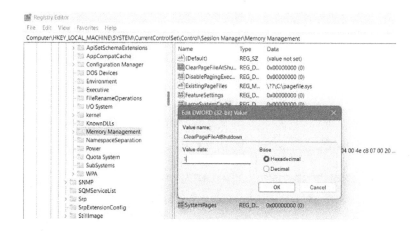

14. Adjust Menu Animations

You can also adjust menu animations to make them look snappier. If you have a slower PC, then faster animations should make it easier to navigate. This is also smooth for the mouse to scroll through.

1. Navigate to the following path.

Computer\HKEY_CURRENT_USER\Control Panel\Desktop

2. Select the "Desktop" key on the left.

3. Find and edit the string value for "MenuShowDelay" from its default value of 400 milliseconds to approximately 200 milliseconds.

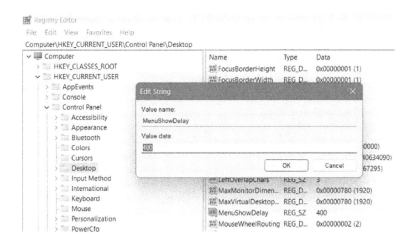

15. Disable Windows Startup Delay

Windows puts a tiny delay on startup to help apps starting up with Windows go through the process smoothly so that you can experience a smooth desktop without lags. However, if you don't have many startup apps, this delay could be unnecessary, and you can disable it.

1. **Go to the following path.**

Computer\HKEY_CURRENT_USER\Software\Microsoft\Windows\CurrentVersion\Explorer

2. **Create a key named** "Serialize" and add a new DWORD (32-bit) value inside it.

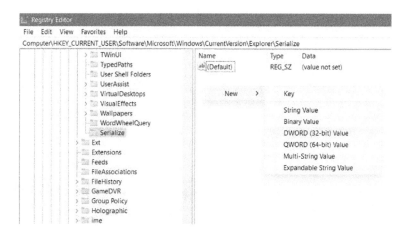

3. **Name it** "StartupDelayInMSec" and set its value to "O." You will see an immediate boost in performance.

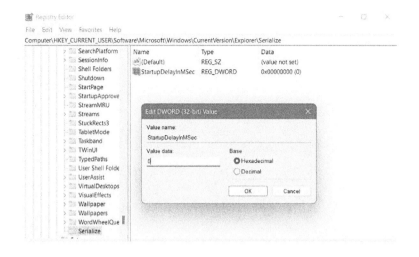

Tip: Don't Microsoft dictate which browser you use to <u>open links in Windows</u>. Here's how to use your favorite option.

16. Remove Bing from Start Menu Search

The Windows 11 Start menu comes with a default Bing search engine. If you're not a big fan of Bing, you may want to remove it from the search box.

1. Navigate to the path as shown below.

Computer\HKEY_CURRENT_USER\Software\P
olicies\Microsoft\Windows

2. Create a new "Explorer" key.

3. Under the created key, add a new DWORD (32-bit) value called "DisableSearchBoxSuggestions."

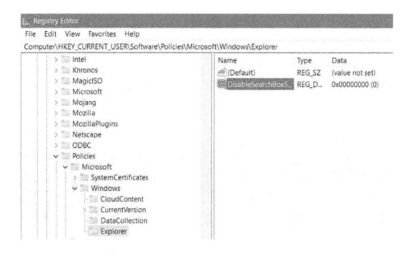

4. Set its value data to "1."

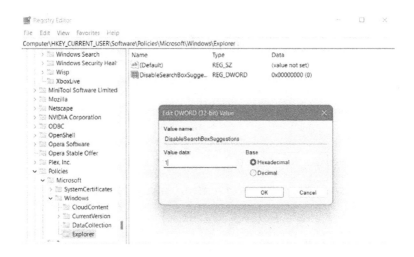

5. After a subsequent PC restart, the Bing search box will be entirely missing from your Windows 11 Start menu.

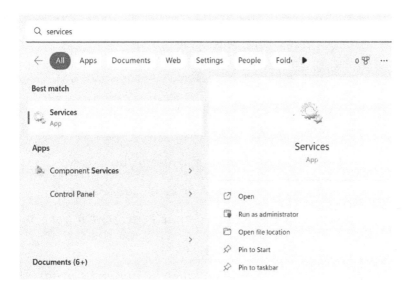

Windows Registry GLOSSARY

common terms related to the Windows Registry that you may encounter in this field:

1. Windows Registry: A hierarchical database that stores configuration settings and options for the Windows operating system and installed applications.

2. Key: A container in the Registry that can hold values, subkeys, and data.

3. Value: A data element stored in a Registry key that defines a setting or configuration option.

4. Data type: The format in which data is stored in a Registry value, such as REG_SZ for a string value or REG_DWORD for a 32-bit integer value.

5. Subkey: A key contained within another key in the Registry, forming a hierarchy.

6. Hive: A logical group of keys, subkeys, and values in the Registry that represent a portion of the system configuration.

7. Registry Editor: The built-in Windows utility used to view and edit the Registry.

8. Registry Cleaner: A third-party tool designed to scan the Registry for invalid, outdated, or unnecessary entries and remove them.

9. Backup: A copy of the Registry made for the purpose of restoring it in case of system errors or data loss.

10. Permissions: Access rights assigned to users or groups that determine their level of access to Registry keys and values.

11. Registry hive file: A file containing a portion of the Registry, saved in a specific format and located in the Windows file system.

www.ingramcontent.com/pod-product-compliance
Lightning Source LLC
LaVergne TN
LVHW052058060326
832903LV00061B/3425